ELSA PUBLISHING

KHMER CUISINE

BY SONG SAA

KATHLEEN BERINGER
PHOTOGRAPHY BY JOERG LEHMANN

ELSA PUBLISHING

"OUR CHEF'S GARDENS
BRING KHMER FLAVOURS
TO LIFE ON THE SONG SAA MENU,
GROWING A RANGE OF
SWEET AND SAVOURY ELEMENTALS
LIKE BIRD'S EYE CHILI, TAI SOI,
AND GALANGAL."

BUN SENG

CONTENTS

10 The Song Saa Crew
14 The Story of Song Saa
   by Kathleen Beringer
16 The Philosophy of Song Saa
20 A Short History of Khmer Cuisine
26 The Map of Cambodia
28 Locally Sourced Food

34 Song Saa Recipes
36 The Pantry
40 Song Saa Sauce Bases

52 Song Saa Breakfast
54 Breakfast Soup Guy Teaw
56 Lemongrass Oatmeal
58 Rice Porridge Bor Bor
60 Hot and Sour Seafood Soup

64 Song Saa Lunch
66 Khmer Rice Cakes
68 Watermelon Salad
70 Courgette and Cucumber Salad
72 Cambodian Mango Salad
74 Soft-Shell Crab Tempura
76 Scallop Ceviche
78 Kampot Pepper Squid
80 Crispy Vermicelli
82 Pad Thai
84 Duck Salad with Black Sesame
86 Lamb Cutlets with Fresh Spinach

114 Song Saa Dinner
116 Fish Amok
118 Prawn Laksa
120 Sea Bass in a Coconut and
    Lime Reduction
122 Red Snapper with Green Curry
124 Red Snapper en Papillote
126 Wok-Fried Chicken with Hot Basil
128 Chicken in Pandan Leaves
130 Beef Lok Lak
132 Pork Ribs with Chili Relish
134 Sweet Pork Belly
136 Coconut-Smoked Rack of Lamb
137 Sautéed Prawns with Chili Relish

144 Song Saa Sweets
146 Roasted Pineapple
148 Sweet Potato Pudding with Tapioca
150 Taro and Sticky Rice Pudding
152 Sweet Treats

156 Song Saa Drinks
158 Song Saa Sunset
158 Classic Song Saa
161 Pimm's Rangoon
161 Basil Beauty
162 Lemongrass Collins
162 Passionate Distillers
165 Cucumber Punch
165 Island Cooler
166 Watermelon Breeze
166 Ginger Tonic
169 Ginger Lemongrass
169 Mango Cooler

174 Index
176 Imprint

THE SONG SAA CREW

THE SONG SAA CREW

THE STORY OF SONG SAA

Song Saa Private Island was born of an unexpected offer. In 2006, Australians Rory and Melita Hunter rented a fishing boat to tour Cambodia's Koh Rong archipelago, a cluster of islands separating Cambodia's Bay of Kompong Som from the Gulf of Thailand. The last stop on their last day was Koh Ouen, a small spit of white sand beach ringing a diluted stand of jungle. The family that lived on the island invited the Hunters to a meal. In between courses, the head of the household asked the Hunters if they wanted to buy the island.

More astonishing than the offer was the fact that the Hunters accepted, walking away from their plans to start a new life in New York City. After a transaction involving a brown paper bag full of money and the Cambodian Navy, the Hunters officially owned Koh Ouen and its neighboring island Koh Bong.

The locals called the two islands "Song Saa", Khmer for "The Sweethearts". The genial nickname masked the state of Koh Ouen and Koh Bong, their jungles cut thin from excessive logging, their waters overfished, the reefs in decline, the beaches blighted with litter.

Every plunge into the unknown brings with it two certainties: hard work and turmoil. So it was for the Hunters as they weathered years of personal and commercial upheaval, from navigating Cambodian government bureaucracy to losing all of their investors during the Great Recession. Throughout, they remained committed to building a showcase for their corner of Cambodia.

My introduction to Song Saa also came from an unexpected offer. My husband, Daniel, received word of an opportunity to invest in a luxury ecotourism resort in Cambodia, working to rehabilitate a pair of islands as well as the local communities. Daniel didn't have time to visit the island, so he asked his father, Kaj, to go. Rory and Melita gave Kaj a tour, laying out their vision when Song Saa was little more than a single building on a deserted island. Kaj, a veteran traveler, returned ecstatic. Daniel, trusting his father's enthusiasm and experience, signed on to the adventure without setting foot on Koh Ouen.

At last, in 2011, the Hunters oversaw the opening of their dream, Song Saa Private Island. Twenty-four open-plan villas poised over the water with magnificent views of the gulf or the bay, or hidden throughout the thick, replenished jungle. White sand beaches, pristine waters, and restored tropical reefs. Building materials sourced locally, with thatched roofs for the villas and recycled timber from driftwood, old fishing boats, and derelict factories on the mainland. Art and furniture created by local artists or acquired in provincial markets.

The following year, I visited Cambodia for the first time with Daniel and our children. Our first two days in Siem Riep also gave me my first taste of Khmer food. Every dish was delicate, fresh, and delicious – so good, in fact, I was surprised I'd never heard about Cambodian cuisine.

Then we went to Song Saa.

There's nothing like a first impression. The boat ride from the pier at Sihanoukville to Song Saa takes about 45 minutes. I was more excited every minute of the trip, watching the mainland recede, then being out on open water, wondering what this new world would look like. Finally, outlines appeared on the horizon – palms and coconut trees, then huts. As we neared the pier on Song Saa, I saw about 15 staff dressed in white and waving welcome. Everything melded into a tableau as we got closer, the beauty of the island against a sapphire sky and emerald sea, the architecture, the smell of salt and burned wood in the air. I was filled with pure and deep enchantment.

From the moment we stepped off the boat, we took off our shoes and enjoyed what Song Saa calls "barefoot luxury" for the remainder of our stay. Although Koh Ouen is a tiny island, every barefooted step I took amazed me with pure poetry and beauty.

And then there was the food! More of the delicate, fresh fare I'd had in Siem Riep. I was again astonished that no one outside Cambodia seemed to know of Khmer cuisine.

My husband is now the owner of Song Saa Private Island, and I've made many trips since that first breathtaking visit. The only things that have changed have made the experience better. Rory and Melita's commitment to conservation-based luxury tourism remains, a Song Saa Foundation created to further the work with surrounding villages and the environment to improve local livelihoods. A footbridge connects Koh Ouen and Koh Bong, spanning Cambodia's first Marine Reserve safeguarding the reefs and marine life.

The idea to write a book came to me a few years ago, when I took one of the cooking classes Song Saa offers. On a more recent trip, I discovered the food has gotten even better. I decided that now is the time.

Khmer cuisine is incredible, more subtle and balanced than Thai and Vietnamese, never overwhelmed with heat or spiciness. Khmer meals allow the palate to detect and enjoy all of a dish's different compliments. It's better than any other Asian food I've had.

In these pages I want to share Khmer's beautiful, unknown cuisine and its ancient and complex heritage. I hope that you, and as many people as possible, will find as much pleasure in these dishes as I have – a taste of the enchantment I discovered at Song Saa and have never lost.

KATHLEEN BERINGER

THE PHILOSOPHY OF SONG SAA

So much life along the coast of Cambodia surrounds the water and nature. In Koh Rong, colourful houses sit perched over water; locals ready to fish. Further inland, women kayak through watery lotus fields that stretch as far as you can see, gathering supplies. During the hottest months of the year, the mainlanders have these fields as their own ocean of pink and white blossoms, in contrast to the archipelago's white sand beaches and bright blue waters. Capturing this sense of place is so important.

The people of Koh Rong are justifiably proud of the area they have helped regenerate. When we arrived in Cambodia, so much of the land and water was becoming unusable and unsustainable. The area lacked opportunity but the potential of place and people was undeniable.

Deciding to build and regenerate this place involved asking the question: How do we move beyond building a resort to building a place where people, land, and water all help regenerate each other? The evolution of Song Saa became the evolution of place and people.

Ten years on, Koh Rong's local economy flourishes far beyond the presence of Song Saa. Locals take care of what is now one of the largest Marine National Parks in South-East Asia. And it takes care of them, providing an abundance of food and other marine life. Each ecosystem, from the people, to the forests, to the beaches, builds resilience in one another.

For anyone who has visited Song Saa, that harmony can be felt in every experience, and especially in the food. Food has this magical ability to weave a sense of place into every dish – the history, culture, stories, memories, and care that goes into each one. I'm so grateful that these recipes capture this. The feeling that the sea is nearby, the colours and beauty of the local markets, the welcoming feeling of family-style eating.

I hope you enjoy these recipes and the spirit of Song Saa, the appreciation and care for people and place, as much as I have.

Melita Koulmandas

MELITA KOULMANDAS

WELCOME

A SHORT HISTORY OF KHMER CUISINE

No one should be surprised to discover that rice and fish exert enormous influence on Cambodia's Khmer cuisine. According to Chan Sarun's book "10 Main Rice Crops", Khmer ancestors began growing rice at least 4000 years ago. Today, the Genebank at the International Rice Research Institute holds 4,895 rice seed varieties from Cambodia. Perhaps most telling, K. Helmers explains in "Rice Production" in Cambodia that "the English phrase 'to eat' is 'pisa' bei in Khmer, which literally means 'eat rice.'"

During the monsoon season, from about May to October, verdant grass and luxuriant jungle form islands among the sweeping floods that habour deep and shallow rice paddies. This is when Cambodians cultivate numerous varieties of premium fragrant jasmine rice like Phka Romdoul, its strong floral aroma and tender texture after cooking earning it the title of world's best rice four times in the past eight years.

Downpours swell the Mekong River that cuts Cambodia in half, the surge sending water through the Tonle Sap River into Tonle Sap Lake, near the capital. UNESCO calls the Tonle Sap "the most extensive freshwater lake in South-East Asia". More than 200 fish species navigate the basin formed by the Tonle Sap, Mekong, and Bassac rivers, making the Tonle Sap "one of the top four fishery production areas in the world".

The lakes, rivers, and wetlands in Cambodia's 25 provinces shape the nation's geographic and culinary landscapes, yet Khmer cuisine encompasses so much more than these two staples.

The rise of the Khmer Empire in the early ninth century turned the area around Phnom Penh into a commercial hub. Arab, Chinese, and Indian ships carried international traders up the Mekong River, bringing the traders' foreign cuisines with them.

Indians brought spices like turmeric and curries. As a distinct Vietnamese culture arose to the east and the Ayutthaya Kingdom that became Thailand arose to the west, both made contributions to Angkor's culinary traditions. The Portuguese and Spanish arrived in the 16th century, adding New World foods like peanuts and potatoes. When Cambodia become a French protectorate in 1863, the French transported their baguettes, beer, coffee, chocolate, onions, carrots, and broccoli from Mediterranean ports to the Mekong Delta.

Cambodia's native ingredients are likewise rich and varied. Pepper from Kampot Province has been "revered by gourmands worldwide for its floral and eucalyptus notes, its heady aroma, its musky heat, and its medicinal properties". The European Union accorded Kampot pepper a protected geographic indication in 2016.

Palm sugar obtained from the sap of the palm sugar flower in Kampong Speu Province doesn't need refining, thereby retaining its "very rich aromas of honey, eucalyptus, and coconut". The sugar earned its geographical indication from the EU in 2017.

Wild honey harvested from the wild Asian giant honeybee in Mondulkiri Province is praised for its "aromatic smell and light sweet taste from the nectars of a variety of wild Cambodian medicinal plants". Gathered responsibly by the indigenous people of the rainforest, this is the honey you'll find here on Song Saa.

A mild climate and fertile soil have earned Battambang Province the title of "rice bowl of Cambodia". Those welcoming conditions also yield oranges considered for a third geographical indication, as well as vibrant, musky turmeric and earthy, sweet saffron.

These are a few of the local aromatic and pungent resources that combine with flavours like lime juice, soy, fish, and oyster sauces to create the fundamental tastes, of and condiments for, Khmer dishes. Kroeung, a spicy paste made from lemongrass, galangal, turmeric, kaffir lime, and garlic, provides the elementary note in dishes that frequently end with the word "kroeung". Made in royal and individual varieties, it might be green from the lemongrass, or yellow because of extra turmeric, or red thanks to the addition of dried chili pods.

The mangrove swamps of Cambodia's "rainforest by the sea" in our own Koh Kong Province are home to fish, shrimp, prawns, crabs, shellfish, and snails. Salted and fermented river fish are ground into a greyish-brown fish paste to make the national staple known as prahok, used as a seasoning or condiment to provide depth in a meal. One writer dubbed prahok "the secret ingredient of Cambodian cuisine". So pungent it's often referred to as "Cambodian cheese" – think Limburger, not Chèvre – it's usually accompanied by a warning to tourists about being "an acquired taste".

Despite these profound flavours, Khmer cuisine impresses the palate with its nuances. Cambodian chef Kethana Dunnett has entertained guests like Gordon Ramsay and Luke Nguyen at her Sugar Palm restaurant in Siem Riep. She told me, "There is a uniqueness to Khmer cuisine despite the similarities with food from our neighbouring countries – in particular, the extensive use of fresh herbs to construct subtle flavours. We try to have the herbs as primary flavour along with aromatic spices, rather than strong spices such as chili, so there is less spice in Khmer food compared to food in Thailand and Laos."

Cambodian meals are typically served as three or four little dishes with rice and a soup alongside. On top of the huge selection of fresh fish, rice, and diverse herbs and spices, green vegetables in soups, stir-fries, and salads make up a large portion of the local diet. Pickled vegetables are another vital component, and unripe fruit add crisp, savoury notes to salads.

Dishes are fresh and light, never fatty nor oily, the flavour always a balance between sweet, sour, salty, and bitter. What's more, homegrown ingredients often cut the distance of "farm-to-table" down to "backyard-to-table".

Our chef's gardens bring those flavours to life on the Song Saa menu, growing a range of sweet and savoury elementals like bird's eye chili, tai soi, and galangal. The island provides bounties of banana leaves, jackfruit, jambolan, and tamarind. We source coconuts, cashew nuts, and select pork products from Koh Rong. And the waters all around provide barracuda, blue swimmer crabs, squid, and our own Song Saa sea salt.

In Cambodian culture, emphasis on an oral family tradition and using ingredients close at hand means tourists often find the same meals prepared differently among the provinces. Attempting to identify the country's national dish encounters the same contrasts, a Google search returning a handful of answers. Nevertheless, one dish stands out as the most popular: Fish Amok. Dunnett described it to me as "essentially a steamed curry that, with the addition of an egg, evolves into a soufflé-style curry".

Also known as Amok Trey or Amok Trei, it is considered a special occasion dish among Cambodians. Mekong catfish or snakehead usually provide the heart of the meal, but the amok chouk variation uses snails caught in rice paddies. The egg confers a custardy consistency, or it might be soupy depending on where you add it. The only consistent features of a genuine Fish Amok are that it's served in a banana leaf bowl, and when prepared properly, it is fantastic.

Our goal with this book is to introduce you to the refined, immersive tastes of Cambodian cuisine, emphasizing its variety while helping adventurous cooks find solid ground. What better place to find your feet than with our version of this indispensable Khmer meal: Fish Amok, Song Saa style!

A SHORT HISTORY OF KHMER CUISINE

THE MAP OF CAMBODIA

LOCALLY SOURCED FOOD

The following food items are all sourced from the local communities on the islands surrounding Song Saa. We work closely with our suppliers to ensure that the ingredients are being grown and harvested in a sustainable manner, which does not adversely impact the environment. The foods we source and the ways in which they are created are outlined in this book. This chapter is broken down into sections referring to products we are able to source from the communities within the archipelago, those we can create ourselves on Song Saa and specialty products that certain parts of Cambodia are famous for and that we use, as well the products that we obtain from markets on the mainland.

SUPPLIED FROM KOH RONG ARCHIPELAGO COMMUNITIES

Coconut

All of the coconuts that we serve within the resort are sourced from the trees on the Song Saa islands themselves or from the local community of Prek Svay. As coconut trees only produce a crop after ten years, the trees are fully mature before they can be harvested, which reduces the chance of damaging them whilst retrieving the nuts. The nuts are collected by either climbing the tree to cut them down or by using a large, hooked pole to pull them down to the ground. Neither of these processes incurs any damage to the tree or the surrounding vegetation. Coconuts are one of the major cash crops for the local communities and therefore the groves of trees are well managed and cared for. The coconut is an extremely versatile product and here at Song Saa we are able to use it in drinks, cocktails, desserts and local curries.

Coconut Oil

Using the coconuts grown within the community, a small number of families are able to process the flesh of the coconut into oil. This is then put to use by our spa team in a number of the treatments that they offer. Coconut milk and cream are also separated out and both can be used in the resort's kitchens.

Barracuda

As these fish are active predators they can be targeted specifically by hook and line. This means that any non-target or inappropriately sized individuals can be released unharmed. We have developed a partnership with a small number of fishermen who are willing to fish in this manner, and so we are able to not only set size limits for the fish that we will accept, but also to provide education on the benefits of sustainable fishing.

Bamboo Straws

The only straws that we use in the resort are crafted from locally sourced and harvested bamboo. Even before the resort had opened, staff had observed that members of the local community were using this variety of bamboo as a straw, for example when they were drinking coconuts away from the village. The resort adopted this practice for all of the drinks served on site, the side benefit being the capacity to provide a new source of income to one of the local families, who supply the straw material to Song Saa Private Island. As the bamboo is a fast-growing plant that is found throughout the islands and the resort is the only large-scale user of it, there is little chance of it being overexploited.

Cashew Nuts

The sandy soils found throughout the neighbouring island of Koh Rong are ideal for the development of cashew nut trees. Around March the fruit and the nuts are ready to pick. This harvest provides a valuable source of income to the local communities, and our resort with a sustainable local product. The fruit is sought after within the community and due to its sour flavour is often included in a dipping mixture comprised of salt, sugar and chili.

LOCAL FOOD

Selected Pork Products

Because the Song Saa Foundation has been able to provide several families within the local community with assistance and support in regards to animal husbandry practices, they have been able to increase the output and quality of their pork products. We are also able to support them through the provision of food scraps to feed their animals. With this increased output, they are able to provide whole animals to the resort's kitchen. Our remaining requirements are met by select farmers from the Kampong Saom province on the mainland.

Squid

The squid in this area are most commonly caught by small-scale operations that use hook and line techniques. As the lures used are produced specifically for squid, there is near zero by-catch. It is also a good species to target as squid are a fast-growing, short-lived species, which helps reduce the possibility of over fishing. They are targeted at night, often off small polystyrene boats in coastal areas.

Blue Swimmer Crab

This species of crab is the most commonly found species within Cambodian waters. Although sometimes observed within coral reefs, it is more regularly found on the sandy seafloor. As they are caught using baited crab pots or traps, they are brought ashore alive, thereby allowing gravid (egg-bearing) females or juveniles to be returned to the water. As the traps are designed specifically to attract and hold crabs there is minimal by-catch, although any that is created can also be returned live to the water. They provide a wonderful sweet meat and we often serve the crabs whole as a part of our seafood BBQ dining experience or turn the meat into delicious crab cakes.

LOCALLY SOURCED FOOD

CREATED ON SONG SAA

Assorted Herbs
Within the Song Saa grounds we have a chef's garden. This space includes a number of vegetable beds that provide produce for our Culinary Journey experience. They also provide the resort's kitchens with a range of herbs, freshly picked to order. These fresh ingredients include tai soi, mizuna, bird's eye chili, laska leaves, lemongrass, galangal and mint.

Banana Leaves and Flowers
Although not eaten, the leaves are extremely useful in cooking as they are used to wrap chicken and fish dishes before they are baked or grilled on a BBQ. The soft inner petals – the flower – can be used in salads as well as a wrapping, when boiled, for chicken Khmer sausage.

Jackfruit
These large fruit are grown on Song Saa Private Island and can be used in both sweet and savoury dishes. As a part of our traditional Khmer menu they are used in the Khmer soup known as koko. It can also be used in curries and made into a pickle.

Papaya
Due to the heavy seasonality of many fresh ingredients, it is common in many Asian cuisines to use certain fruit while they are still green. Within the Khmer cooking undertaken at Song Saa, we use the locally grown green papaya in a traditional salad.

Morinda Fruit
The leaves of this plant are available year around and are served as a complement to the traditional Khmer dish of amok. As this is a fast-growing tree that grows well in sandy soils, the harvesting of a small number of its leaves does not harm the plant.

Melastoma
This is a beautiful local flower that is found on the Song Saa islands. The purple petals are edible and are used as a garnish in the resort's salads.

LOCAL FOOD

Jambolan & Maprang
Jambolan, a plum-like fruit, ripens in May. It can be served whole or made into jam. Maprang is used to make sweet and sour snacks (in season in April).

Tamarind
Tamarind is a sour-flavoured root that is used to make a stock or is crushed down for use in various marinades. Here on Song Saa the root is seasonal and therefore only available in December.

FROM SPECIAL REGIONS

There are a number of regional specialty ingredients that our chefs have studied and sourced from all over Cambodia. Wherever possible, we aim to purchase our foodstuffs from domestic sources and ideally from as close as possible to Sihanoukville, the nearest mainland town.

Kampot Pepper
Kampot pepper is world-renowned for its full but mild flavour. Produced on the mainland, in the nearby province of Kampot, the combination of climate and soil type help produce the perfect growing conditions for this spice. As this crop is protected under a geographical indication scheme, there are strict controls over the varieties of plants used as well as the assurance that the crop is produced organically.

Ibis Rice
The sole variety of rice served in the resort, ibis rice is produced by farmers who have committed to protecting and monitoring the waterfowl population in their part of northern Cambodia. Of particular importance is the giant ibis, which is Cambodia's national bird and is recognised internationally as critically endangered. Entering the scheme, farmers agree to set aside key areas of their land to be maintained as suitable habitat for the birds as well as to farm in an environmentally and bird-friendly manner. In return, they are paid a premium price for their crop.

LOCALLY SOURCED FOOD

Honey
The honey that is used within the resort is sourced from sustainable producers from Mondulkiri province of northeast Cambodia. As the honey is produced within the lush rainforest still found in this region, the bees have access to a wide range of plants, which give the honey its unique flavour. By working with local producers and providing them with a sustainable forest-sourced income, the pressure to destroy the forest for other users is reduced.

FROM THE LOCAL MAINLAND

Fresh Fruits and Vegetables
Between 85 and 90% of the produce that we use on a regular basis is sourced from local markets. Of the remaining produce, some is sourced or produced on the islands of the archipelago, with only a small percentage imported from elsewhere. Depending on the season, this can be as little as 10% of the fresh produce order. The imported items are only those unable to be grown locally.

Poultry
The chicken, duck and quail used on the island are all sourced from local farmers from the areas around Sihanoukville. The small-scale operations that characterise Cambodian farming not only help create better living conditions for the animals, but also ensure that when buying from these producers delete we are supporting local families.

Seafood
For the seafood products that cannot be sourced from local communities, the resort purchases from the markets in Sihanoukville. As this market deals solely with locally caught species it again helps support local fishermen as well as reducing the greenhouse impact of transportation.

Samai Rums
One night, Daniel Pacheco and Antonio Lopez de Haro wondered why Cambodia, with such an abundance of sugarcane and molasses, was not producing its own premium rum. They create hand-crafted, premium rums using high-quality, locally grown ingredients and a process that pays tribute to age-old rum-making traditions. Samai rums are complex and full of character, displaying a flavour profile that reflects the uniqueness of the Cambodian terroir.

SONG SAA RECIPES

THE PANTRY

ESSENTIAL TOOLS

Food processor
Immersion blender
Mandoline
Nonstick pan
Pestle and mortar
Wok

TINNED GOODS

Coconut cream
Coconut milk
Vegetable stock

DRY GOODS

Cashew nuts
Fried shallots Jasmine rice
Grated coconut
Jasmine rice
Pad thai noodles
Peanuts
Sticky rice
Tapioca
Vermicelli rice noodles

HERBS AND FRESH PRODUCTS

Bird's eye chili
Coriander
Curry leaves (frozen)
Galangal
Garlic
Ginger
Green Kampot peppercorns
Kaffir lime leaves (frozen)
Lemongrass (frozen)
Lime
Long chili
Mint
Pandan leaves (frozen)
Shallots
Spring onions
Thai basil
Turmeric

OILS

Peanut oil
Rapeseed oil
Sesame oil

SAUCES AND CONDIMENTS

Chili paste
Chili sauce
Fish sauce
Hoisin sauce
Ketchup
Oyster sauce
Shrimp paste
Soy sauce
Sweet chili sauce
Sweet soy sauce
Tamarind paste

SWEEETENERS

Palm sugar
Sugar

SPICES

Cinnamon sticks
Coriander seeds
Cumin seeds
Dried chilies
White peppercorns

SONG SAA RECIPES

AT THE FOOD MARKET IN SIEM REAP

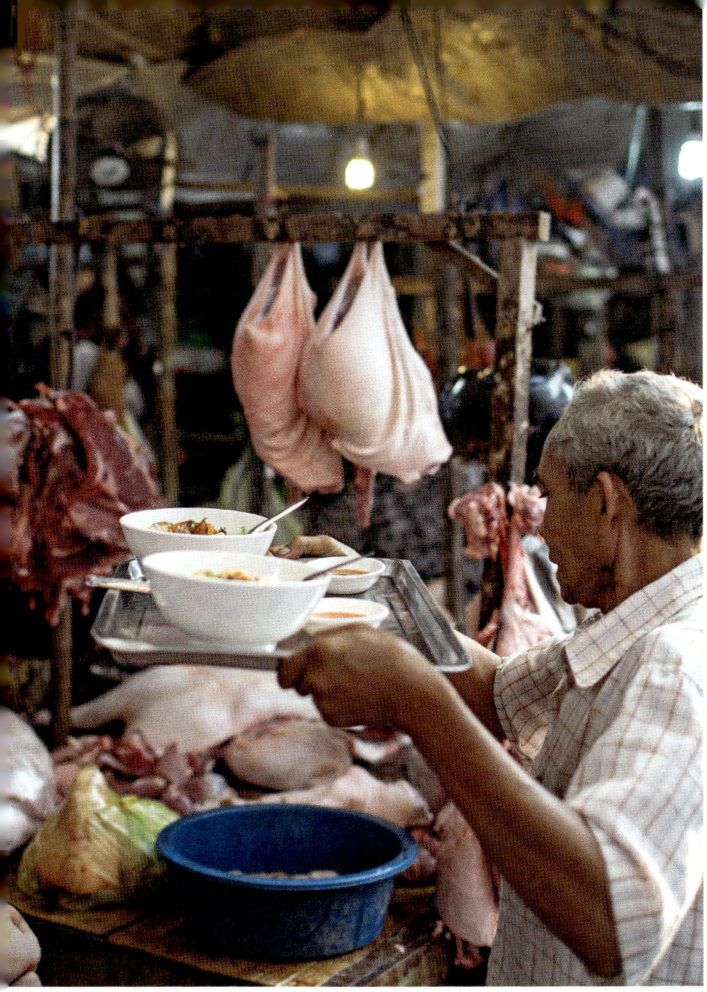

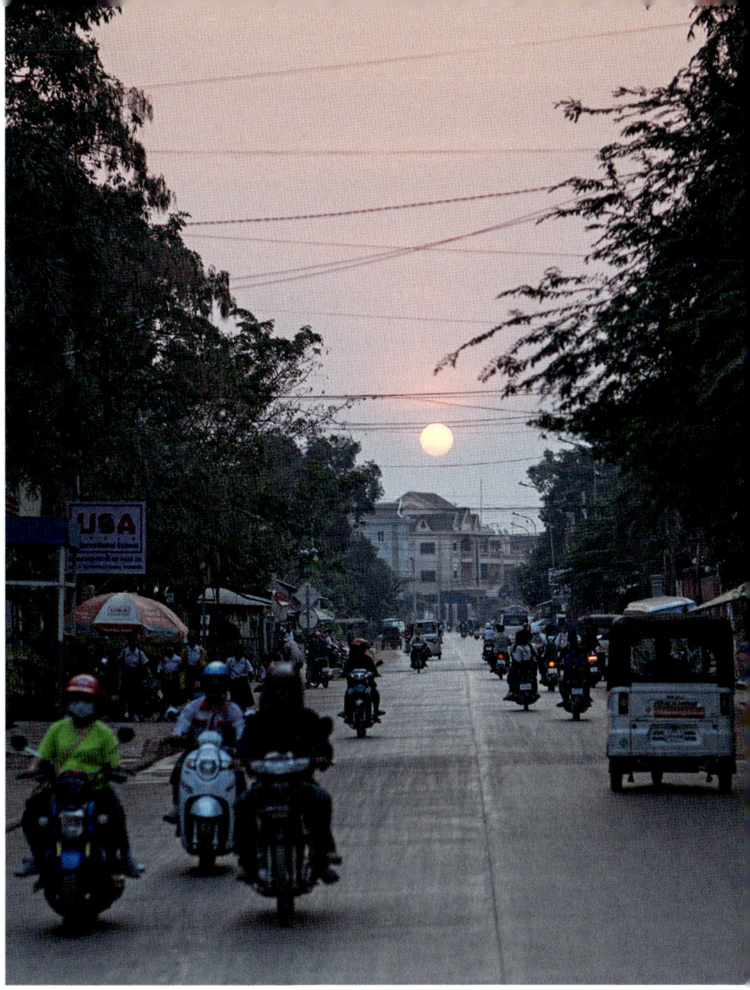
USA

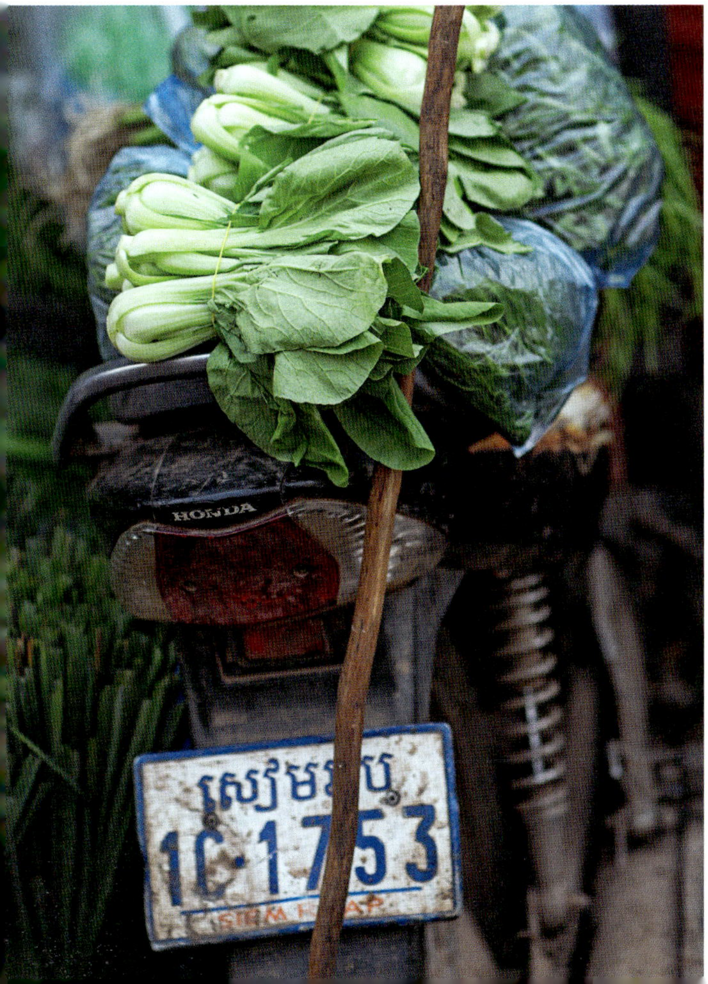
HONDA
1C-1753

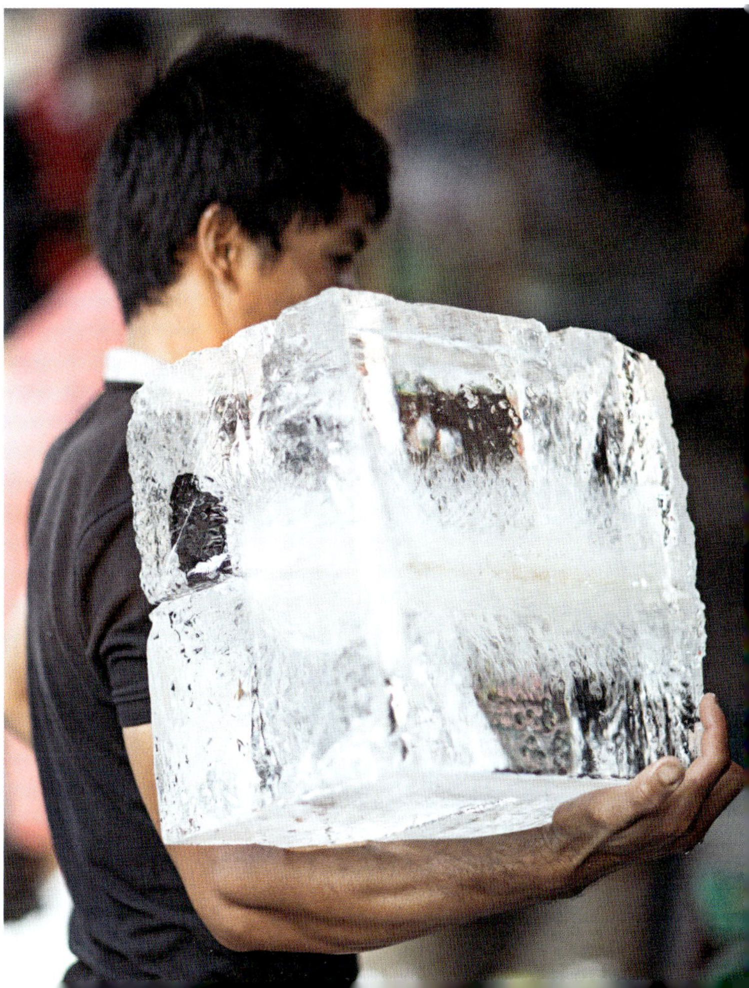

SONG SAA SAUCE BASES

All Bases Serve 4

BIRD'S EYE CHILI RELISH

INGREDIENTS

6 red bird's eye chilies

6 green bird's eye chilies

3 dried chilies

3 long chilies

8 garlic cloves

4 shallots

2 tsp rapeseed oil

1 tsp palm sugar

½ tsp shrimp paste

1 tsp oyster sauce

1 tsp soy sauce

1 tsp fish sauce

METHOD

Cut open all the chilies and remove the seeds with a knife or a spoon. Peel and roughly chop the garlic and the shallots. In a blender, mix the red bird's eye chilies, green bird's eye chilies, dried chilies, long chilies, garlic and shallots. Add a little water (about 2 tablespoons) if necessary. Blend until smooth.

Heat the rapeseed oil in a frying pan, then add the blended paste. Cook over a low heat for 25 minutes. Add the palm sugar, shrimp paste, oyster sauce, soy sauce and fish sauce. Check for seasoning and add more of any of the sauces to taste.

COCONUT LIME REDUCTION FOR SEA BASS

INGREDIENTS

4 stalks lemongrass

1 thumb-sized piece of fresh galangal

4 lime leaves

200 ml (1 ¾ cups) fish stock

800 ml (3 ¼ cups) coconut milk

salt and pepper

Plus

pestle and mortar

METHOD

Cut the lemongrass into 5 cm (2 in) lengths and with a pestle and mortar grind them to a paste. Peel and chop the galangal, add and grind. Keep the lime leaves whole. Put all the ingredients into a saucepan and gently cook for 30 minutes until the sauce has thickened. Continue until you have a smooth paste. Season with salt and pepper before serving.

GREEN CURRY PASTE FOR RED SNAPPER

INGREDIENTS

½ tsp coriander seeds

½ tsp cumin seeds

2 stalks lemongrass

2 tbsp chopped galangal

2 tbsp chopped garlic

2½ tbsp chopped shallots

1 tsp chopped bird's eye chilies

1 tbsp lime zest

2 tbsp chopped coriander roots

1 tbsp white peppercorns

1 tsp shrimp paste (kapi)

Plus

pestle and mortar

METHOD

In a nonstick frying pan, dry-roast the coriander and the cumin seeds, then set aside. Slice the lemongrass.

Using a pestle and mortar and starting at the top of the list, grind and add one ingredient after another or mix in a blender, adding a little water. Grinding by hand will give you the best result but if you don't have time use a blender.

Tip – The curry paste is best used immediately. It will keep for 2 days if stored in a container in the fridge.

SONG SAA RECIPES

42

LAKSA

INGREDIENTS

7 stalks lemongrass

1 thumb-sized piece fresh galangal

3 pieces fresh turmeric

2 shallots

1 head of garlic

1 thumb-sized piece fresh ginger

2 chilies

1 bunch fresh coriander roots

2 tsp chili paste

juice and zest of ½ lime

1 tsp coriander seeds, toasted and ground

2 tsp shrimp paste

2 tins (400 ml each) coconut milk

2 tsp curry powder

2 curry leaves

2 tbsp fish sauce

Plus

pestle and mortar

seafood or vegetables, to serve

METHOD

Chop the lemongrass. Peel and chop the galangal, turmeric, shallots, garlic, ginger and chilies. Clean, trim and chop the coriander roots.

Using a pestle and mortar, pound first the lemongrass, then add and pound or grind, one at a time, the galangal, turmeric, shallots, garlic, ginger and chilies.

Add the chili paste and continue to pound until smooth. Now add the coriander roots, lime zest and half the coriander seeds and continue to pound. Add the shrimp paste and transfer from the mortar to a bowl. Rinse the mortar out with one cup of water, reserving the water.

Take 2 tablespoons of the thick coconut fat from the top of the tins. Heat the coconut fat in a frying pan, add the paste and cook for about 3–4 minutes over a medium heat. Add the water from the mortar and cook for another 5–6 minutes. Add the remaining coriander seeds, curry powder and curry leaves and the coconut milk. Cook for another 5 minutes.

Season with fish sauce and lime juice to taste. Add seafood or vegetables to the sauce to serve.

KAMPOT PEPPER SAUCE

INGREDIENTS

2 tbsp chopped ginger

2 tbsp chopped garlic

1 tsp salt

1 tsp sugar

2 tbsp black Kampot peppercorns

2 tbsp fresh lime juice

METHOD

In a blender, mix all the ingredients, then transfer the sauce to a small, shallow bowl. Serve with beef or other red meat.

AMOK PASTE

INGREDIENTS

80 g (3 oz) lemongrass

1 tsp galangal

3 kaffir lime leaves

1 tsp fresh turmeric

4 garlic cloves

6 shallots

Plus

pestle and mortar

METHOD

To make the paste, use a pestle and mortar to grind the ingredients in the order in which they are listed.

Remove the outer leaves of the lemongrass. Roughly chop the stalks, then put them into the mortar and grind to a paste.

Peel and roughly chop the galangal, chop the kaffir lime leaves and peel and chop the fresh turmeric. Add one ingredient after another to the mortar and continue to grind to a paste.

Peel and roughly chop the garlic and the shallots, add to the mortar and continue to grind to a paste. Grind the paste until it is very smooth.

KHMER PEANUT PASTE

INGREDIENTS

1 red bird's eye chili

2 garlic cloves

1 shallot

1 thumb-sized piece fresh ginger

4 tbsp peanut oil

4 tbsp peanut butter

170 ml (¾ cup) coconut milk

170 ml (¾ cup) chicken stock

1 tbsp fish sauce

1 tbsp soy sauce

1 tsp palm sugar

juice of 1 lime

2 spring onions, to garnish

METHOD

Cut open the chili and remove the seeds with a knife or a spoon. Peel the garlic, shallot and ginger. Finely chop the chili, garlic, shallot and ginger.

In a frying pan, heat the peanut oil and add the chopped ingredients. Cook for 3–5 minutes, stirring all the time, until softened. Add the peanut butter. When it has melted, pour in the coconut milk and the chicken stock. Simmer over a medium high heat for 8–10 minutes, stirring frequently.

Stir in the fish sauce, soy sauce, palm sugar and lime juice. Simmer for another 5 minutes. Trim and chop the spring onions and use to garnish.

Tip – This sauce makes a delicious accompaniment for chicken.

RED KROEUNG

INGREDIENTS

For the paste

4 dried red peppers

3 stalks lemongrass

30 g (1 oz) fresh turmeric

30 g (1 oz) fresh galangal

30 g (1 oz) ginger

2 shallots

8 garlic cloves

4 kaffir lime leaves

½ tsp salt

For the sauce

1 tbsp peanut oil

500 ml coconut milk

2 tbsp palm sugar

1 tbsp fish sauce

1 tbsp soy sauce

juice of ½ lime

METHOD

Soak the dried red peppers in water overnight (the peppers are not very flavoursome but they will give colour to the Kroeung). The next day, drain and pat them dry, cut open and remove the seeds. If the skin is still hard, you may have to peel them.

Trim or peel the lemongrass, turmeric, galangal, ginger, shallots and garlic. In a mortar or in a blender, grind or mix all the paste ingredients, starting with the hardest ingredients at the top of the list which will need more grinding. You may have to add a few teaspoons of water for the blender to work.

Grind or blend each ingredient to a paste before incorporating the next one. Continue until you have a smooth paste.

You can freeze the raw paste or put it in a jar and keep it in the fridge for up to 5 days for future use.

If you are going to use the paste right away, heat a frying pan over medium heat and add the peanut oil. As soon as the pan is hot, add the paste. Cook for 5 minutes, stirring occasionally. Add the coconut milk and bring to a boil, stirring all the time. Reduce the heat to low or medium and simmer for another 10 minutes. Add the palm sugar, fish sauce, soy sauce and lime juice. Simmer for another 2–3 minutes.

Tip – You can fry chicken or other meat on the side and add it to the mixture for the last 2 minutes. Stir well and serve with white rice.

SONG SAA RECIPES

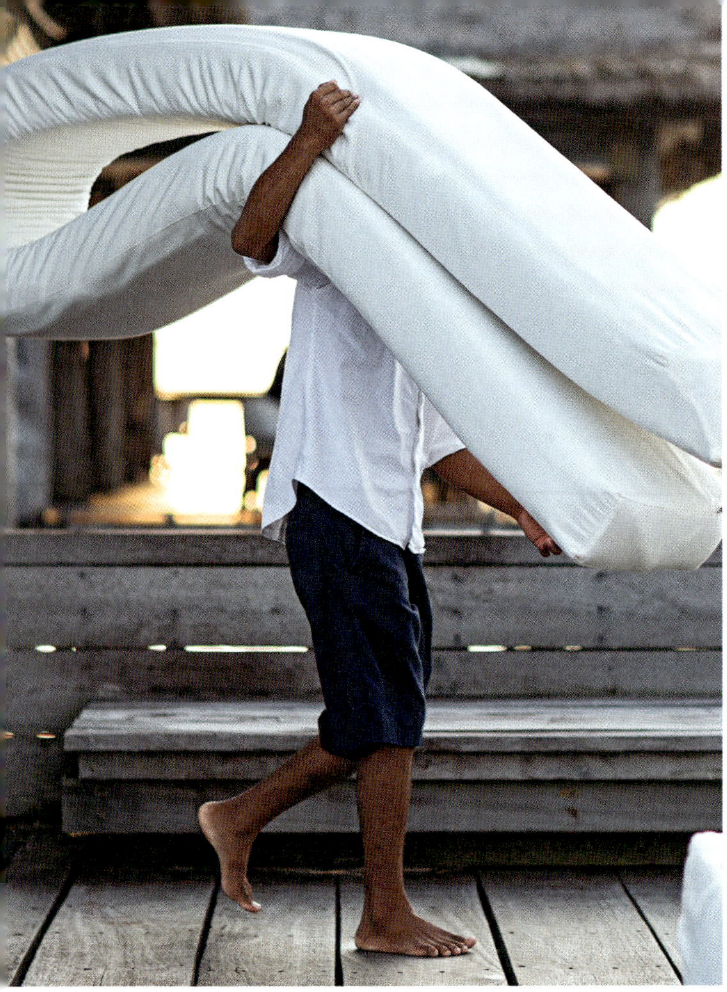
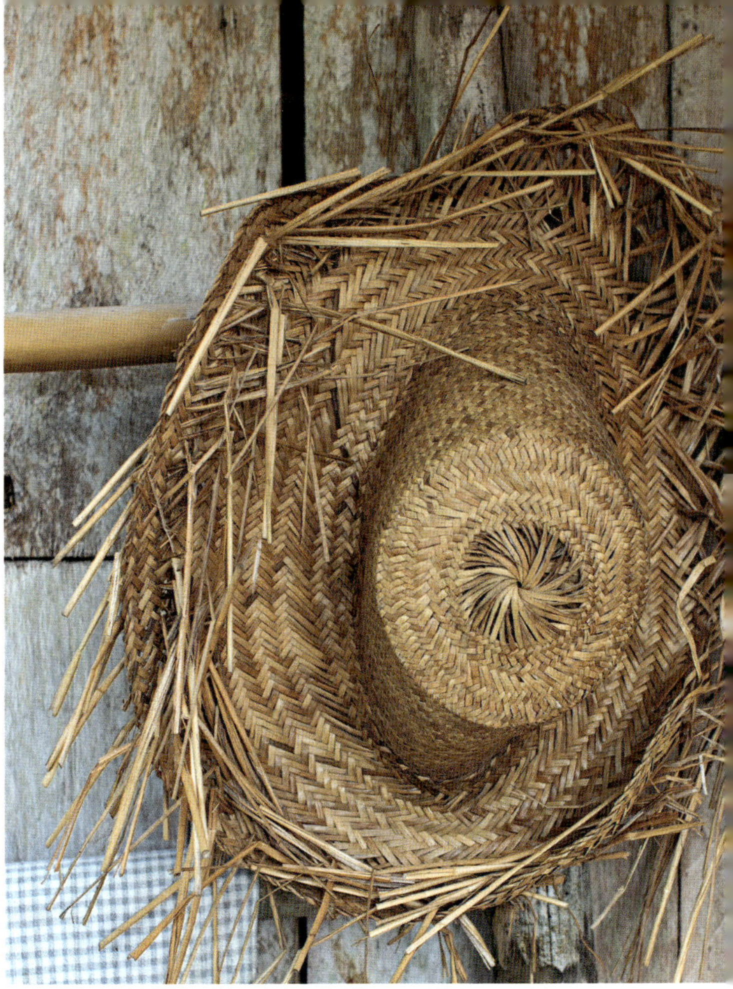
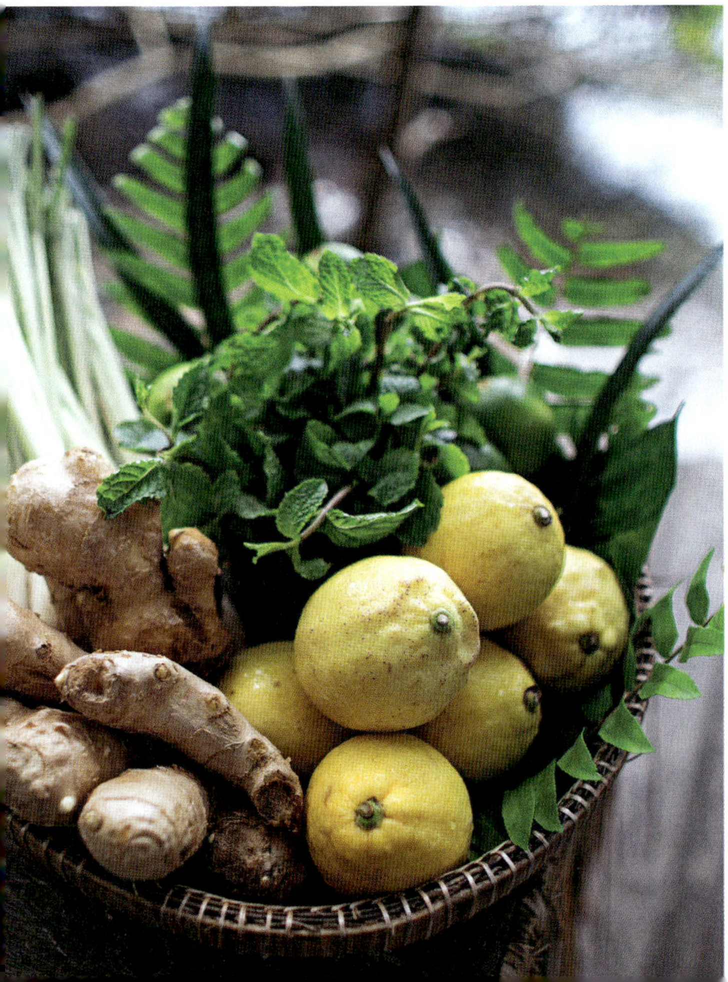
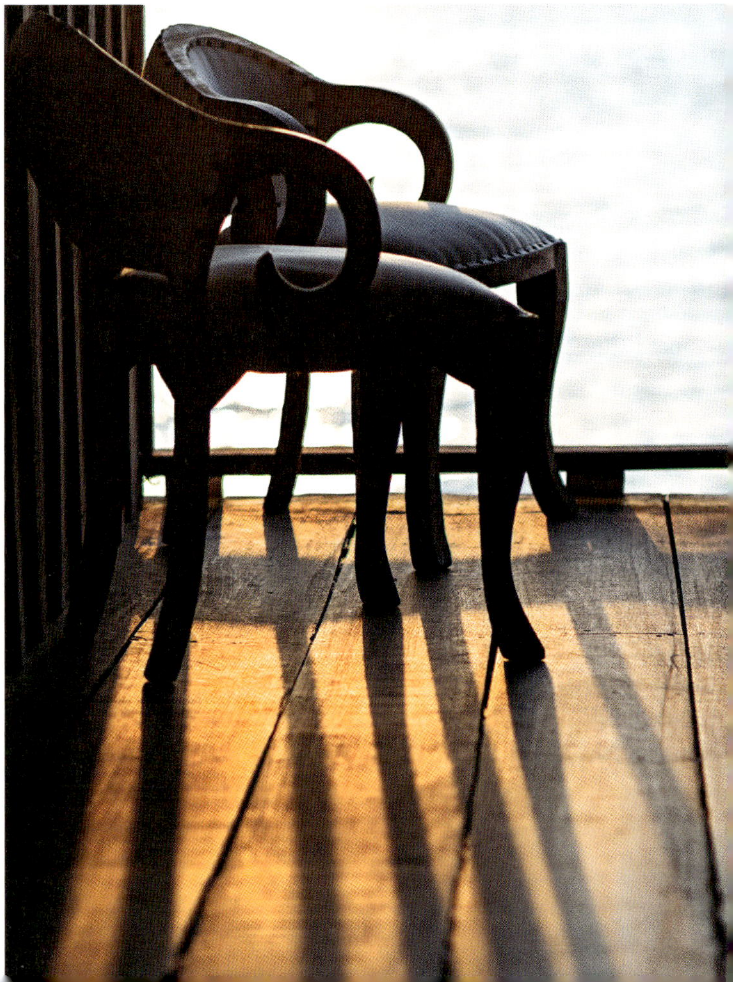

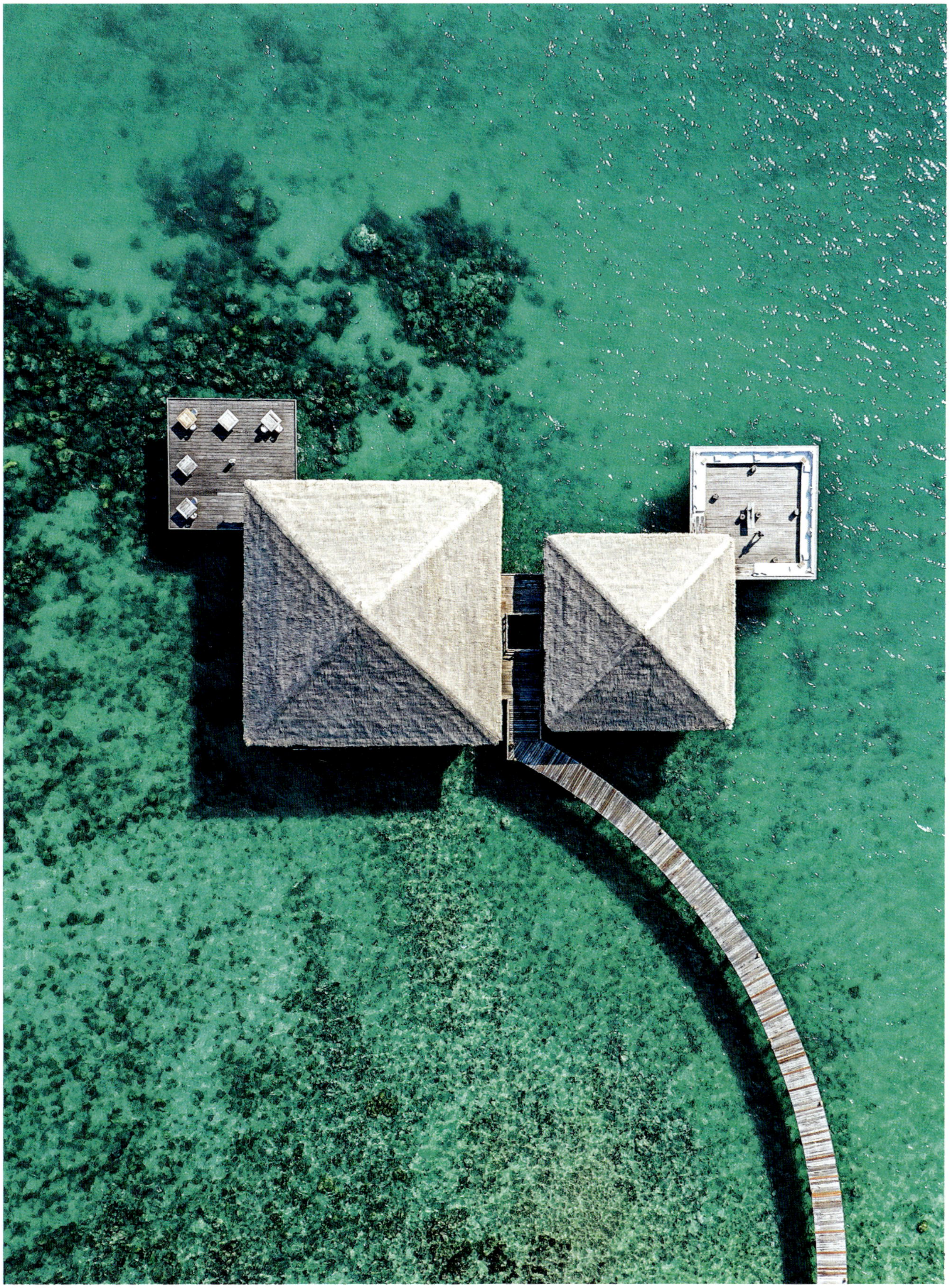

THE BEAUTY OF THE ISLAND, THE SEA, THE SMELL — PURE AND DEEP ENCHANTMENT

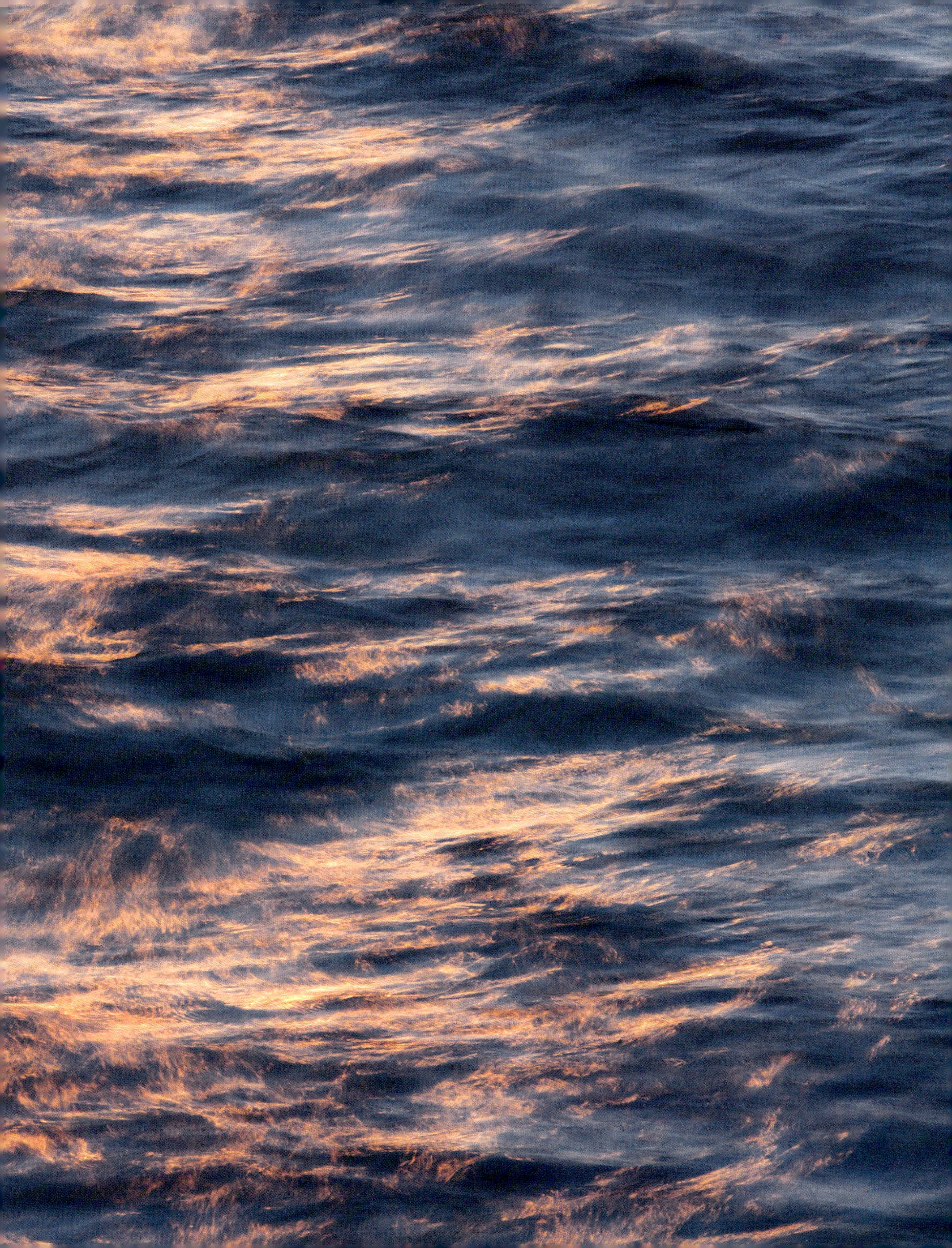

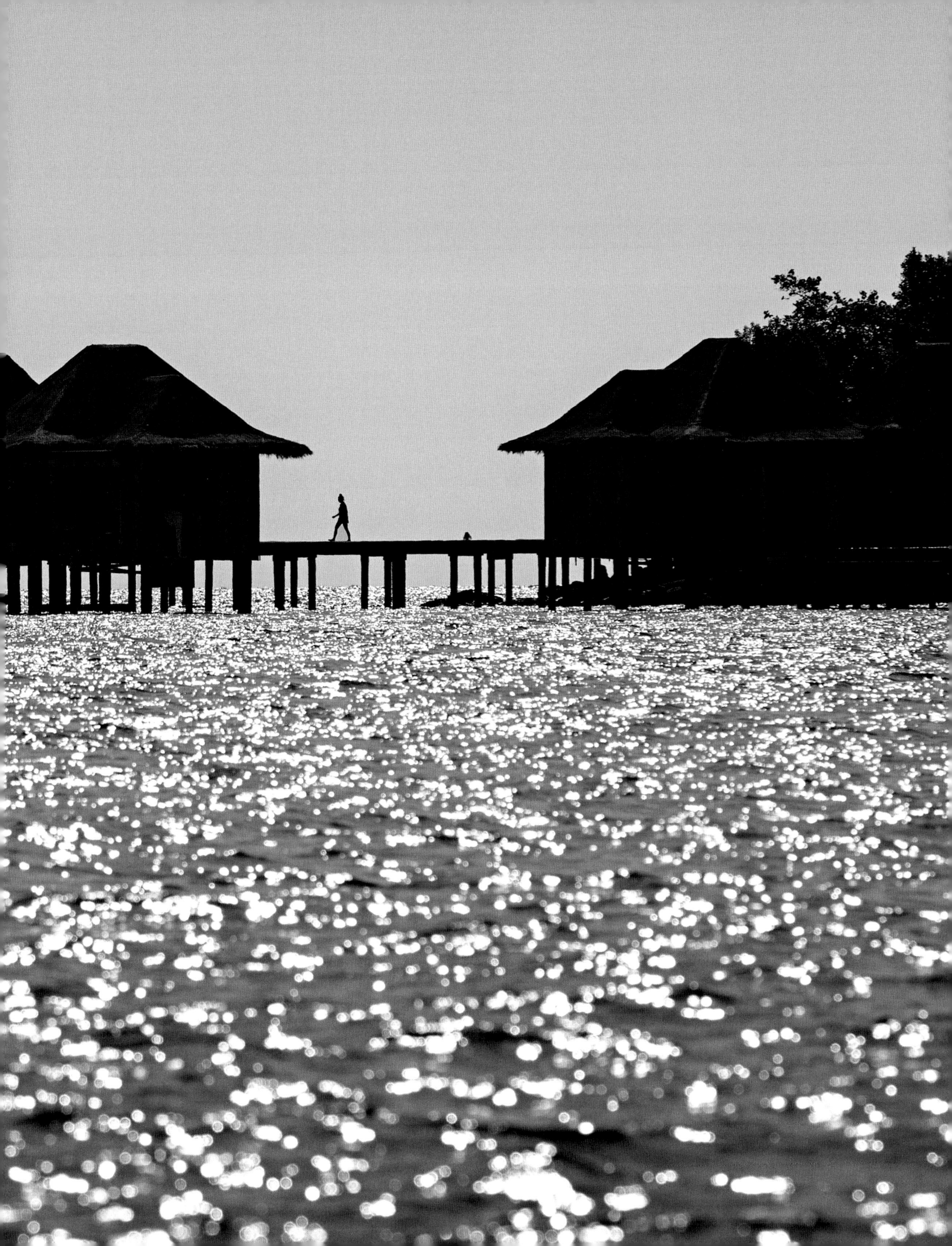

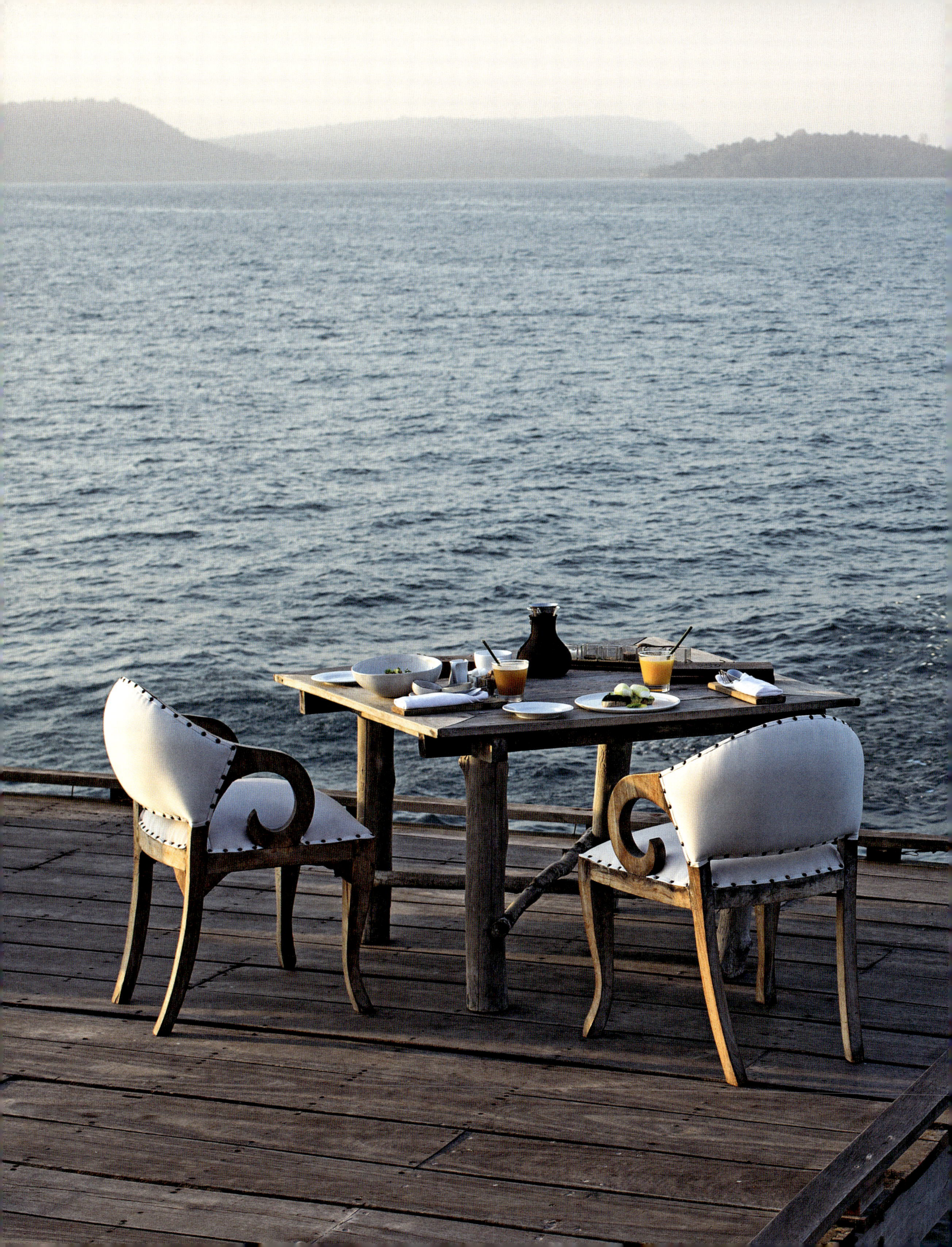

SONG SAA BREAKFAST

BREAKFAST SOUP GUY TEAW

INGREDIENTS / serves 4

200 g (7 oz) rice vermicelli noodles

250 g (9 oz) meat (beef or pork) or vegetables or fish of your choice

300 g (2 cups) mixed vegetables (e.g. broccoli, carrots, pak choi)

2 garlic cloves

5 cm (2 in) piece fresh ginger

2.5 l (10 cups) chicken, pork or vegetable stock

2 tsp fish sauce

2 tsp oyster sauce

2 tsp soy sauce

3 tsp sugar

½ tsp salt

2 tsp chili sauce

1 stalk lemongrass

200 g (1⅓ cups) beansprouts

8 raw prawns or 150 g (1 cup) squid or seafood

TO SERVE

4 tsp fried shallots and/or garlic

4 tsp spring onions

4 tsp fresh coriander

METHOD

Soak the rice vermicelli noodles in water for 1 hour.

Cut the meat (or fish or vegetables) of your choice and the mixed vegetables into small chunks. Peel the garlic and the ginger, chop the garlic.

Put the stock into a saucepan and bring to a simmer. Then add the ginger piece, garlic, fish sauce, oyster sauce, soy sauce, sugar, salt, chili sauce and lemongrass and cook for 5–7 minutes.

Add the beansprouts and the mixed vegetables to the stock and poach for a few minutes, then take them out and set aside. Now add the meat (or fish or vegetables) of your choice and the prawns (or squid or seafood) and poach for 2–4 minutes. Add the vermicelli and cook for 5–6 seconds in the boiling stock, then remove.

Peel, chop and fry the shallots and/or garlic. Chop the spring onions and the coriander. Sprinkle the soup with the fried shallots, spring onions and coriander and serve. Divide the meat (or fish or vegetables), vegetables, prawns (or squid or seafood), beansprouts and vermicelli between four bowls and pour over the hot stock.

SONG SAA BREAKFAST

SONG SAA BREAKFAST

LEMONGRASS OATMEAL

INGREDIENTS / serves 4

1 l (4 cups) full-cream milk

200 ml (1 cup) coconut milk

8 stalks lemongrass

8 kaffir lime leaves

4 cinnamon sticks

4 tsp sugar

200 g (2 cups) dried oatmeal

TO SERVE

4 tsp softened butter

4 pinches cinnamon powder

METHOD

Put the milk, coconut milk, lemongrass, kaffir lime leaves, cinnamon sticks and the sugar into a saucepan and bring to a boil. Reduce the heat and simmer for about 15 minutes for the flavour to develop. Strain the liquid into a clean saucepan and discard the pieces.

Add the oatmeal to the saucepan and bring to a boil again. Reduce the heat and simmer until the oatmeal has been absorbed.

Divide the oatmeal between four bowls and add 1 teaspoon softened butter and a pinch of cinnamon powder to each serving.

RICE PORRIDGE BOR BOR

INGREDIENTS / serves 4

20 g (1½ tbsp) fresh ginger

20 g (1½ tbsp) garlic

20 g (1½ tbsp) dried shrimp

20 g (1½ tbsp) dried squid

40 g (3 tbsp) black mushrooms

400 g (14 oz) meat, seafood or vegetables of your choice (e.g. beef, pork, chicken, fish, prawn, squid, seafood, vegetables)

1.9 l (8 cups) vegetable stock

120 g (½ cup) jasmine rice

4 tbsp cooking oil

2 tsp fish sauce

4 tsp sugar

2 tsp oyster sauce

3 tsp soy sauce

½ tsp pepper

TO GARNISH

fried shallots

chopped spring onions

coriander leaves

METHOD

Peel and chop the ginger and the garlic, chop the dried shrimp and the dried squid. Slice the black mushrooms. Cut the meat or seafood of your choice into 3–4 cm (1½–1¾ in) chunks.

Pour the stock into a saucepan and bring to a boil. Poach the meat or seafood or vegetables for 2–4 minutes. Remove from the heat. Set aside.

Wash the jasmine rice twice. Pour the cooking oil into a saucepan, add the rice, ginger, garlic, dried shrimps, dried squid and mushrooms and sauté everything for 2–3 minutes, stirring all the time, until fragrant but not browned.

Add the cooking liquid and bring to a simmer. Add the fish sauce, sugar, oyster sauce, soy sauce and the pepper.

Reduce the heat and simmer gently for 30–35 minutes.

Divide the soup and the poached meat, seafood or vegetables between four plates. Garnish with fried shallots, spring onions and coriander and serve.

SONG SAA BREAKFAST

SONG SAA BREAKFAST

HOT AND SOUR SEAFOOD SOUP

INGREDIENTS / serves 4

2 stalks lemongrass

30 g (1 oz) fresh galangal

15 g (½ oz) garlic

30 g (1 oz) shallots

1 or 2 red chilies

1 litre (1¾ pints) fish and prawn stock

4 kaffir lime leaves

250 g (½ lb) raw prawns

250 g (½ lb) squid, cleaned

70 g (2½ oz) black mushrooms

1 tsp fish sauce

¼ tsp salt

1½ tsp tamarind paste

½ tsp sugar

TO GARNISH

fresh basil leaves

fresh coriander leaves

1 long chili, chopped

METHOD

Peel or trim, then roughly chop the lemongrass, galangal, garlic, shallots and red chilies. Remove the chili seeds if you donot wish the soup to be too spicy. Crush all the ingredients with a pestle and mortar, adding one ingredient at a time.

In a saucepan, bring the stock to a boil. Add all the crushed ingredients and the kaffir lime leaves as well as the fish sauce, salt, tamarind paste and sugar. Reduce the heat and simmer for 10 minutes.

Bring the stock to a boil again, then add the prawns and squid and black mushrooms. Turn off the heat and poach for 2–4 minutes. As soon as the seafood is cooked take it out and keep warm.

Strain the soup and garnish with the fresh herbs and the chili. Serve with the seafood.

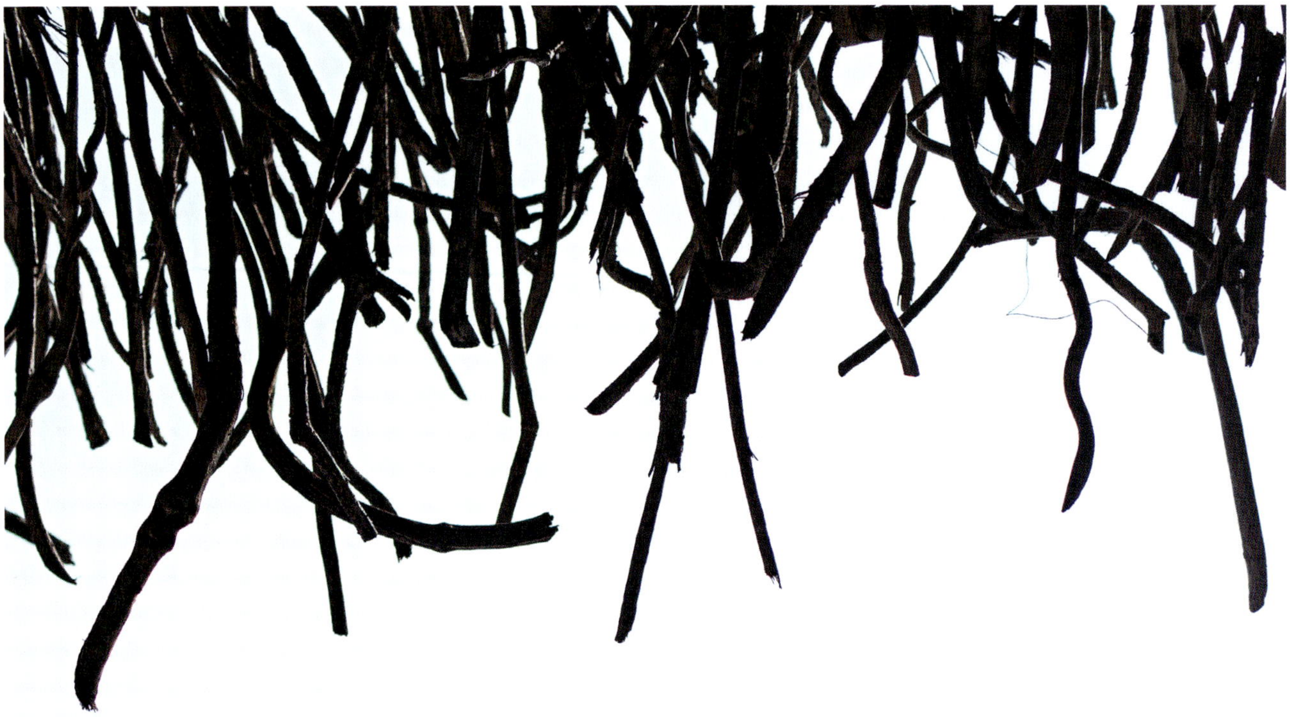

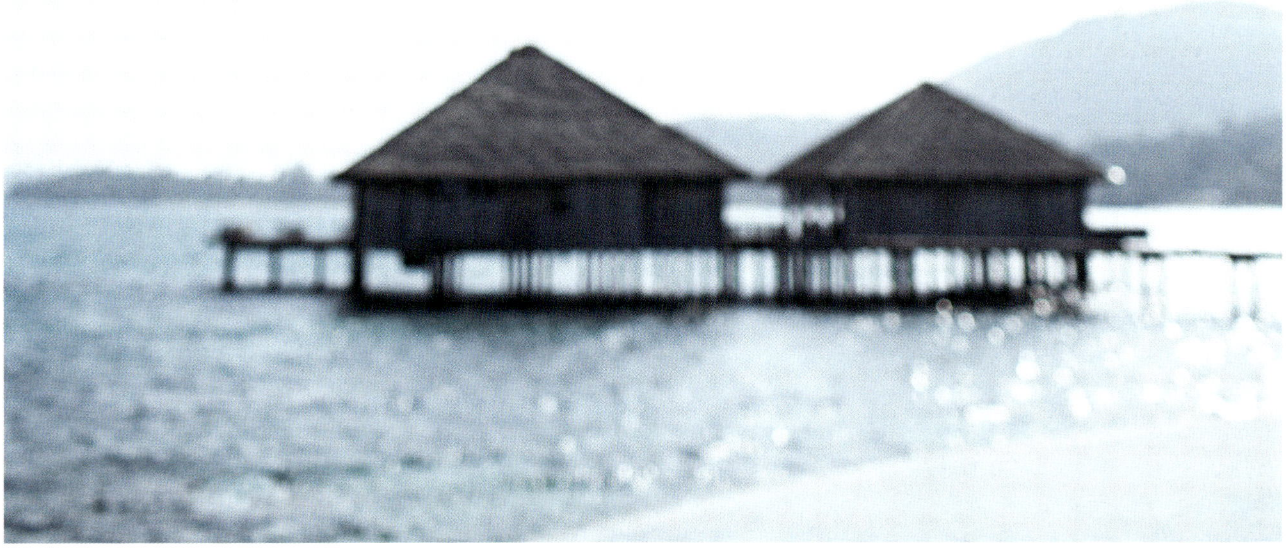

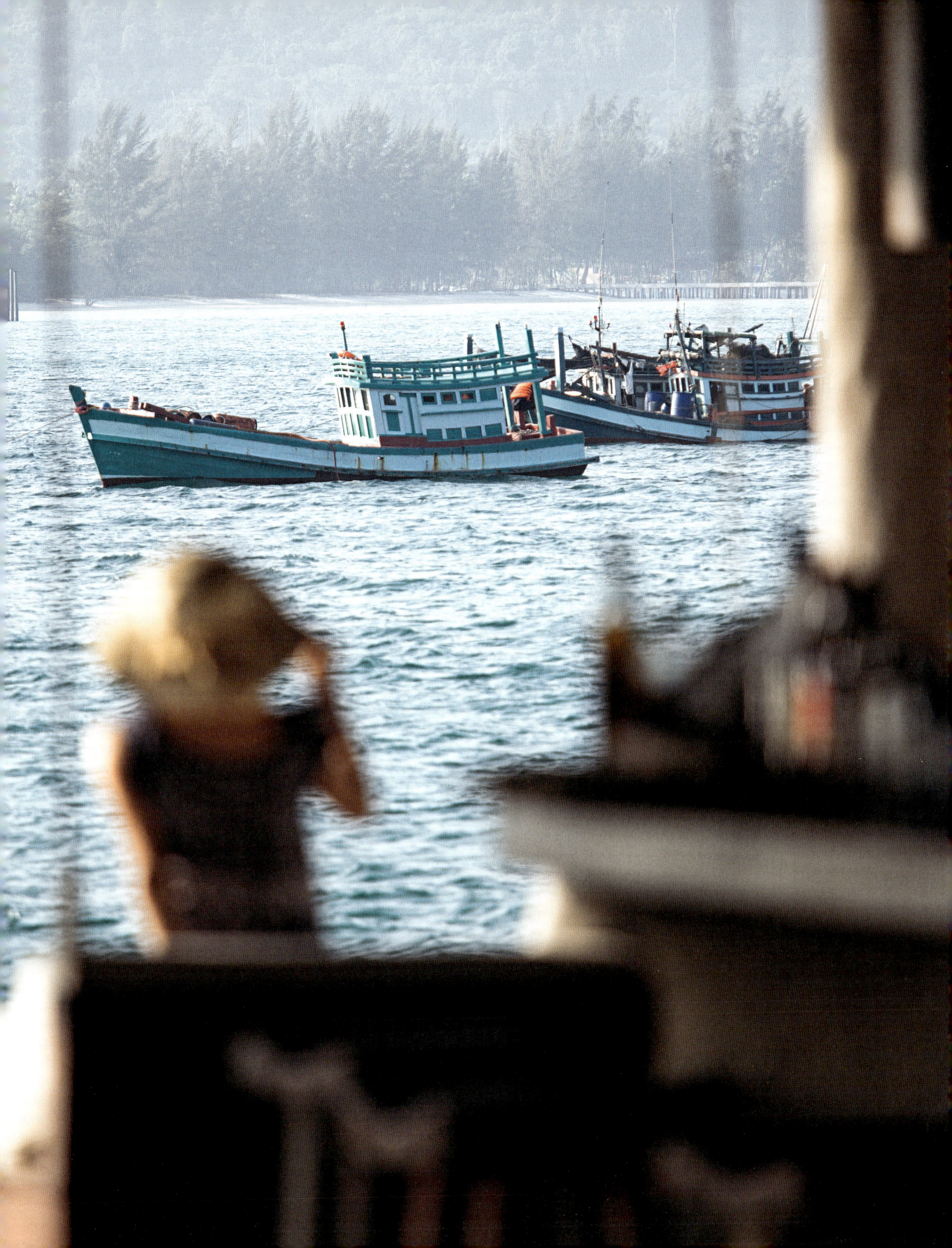

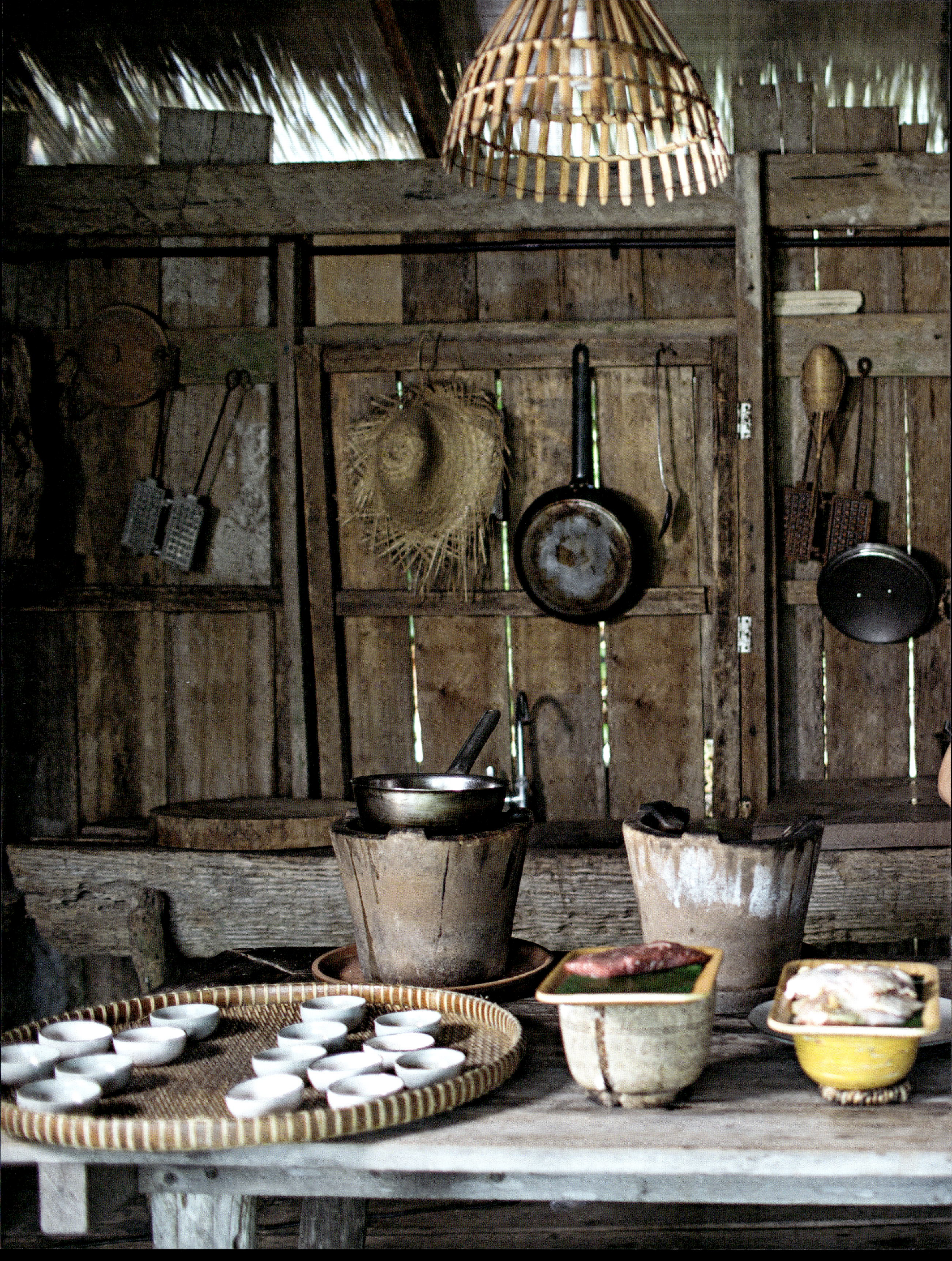

SONG SAA LUNCH

KHMER RICE CAKES

INGREDIENTS / serves 4

For the rice cakes

200 g (1 cup) rice

2 spring onions

200 g (1 cup) rice flour

200 g (1 cup) coconut cream

1 tsp green peppercorns

2 tsp salt

2 tbsp peanut oil

For the dressing

1 garlic clove

½ shallot

½ spring onion

1 carrot

60 g (½ cup) pineapple cubes

1 tbsp palm sugar

100 g fish sauce

2 dried bird's eye chilies

1 tbsp soy sauce

juice of ½ lime

115 g (½ cup) coconut cream

METHOD

To make the dressing, peel and chop the garlic and the shallot. Trim and chop the spring onion. Wash the carrot, then pare off about 16 long strips of peel with a potato peeler.

Put the pineapple cubes in a hot saucepan without fat and cook for 5 minutes, then add the palm sugar and stir until it is dissolved. Add 360 ml (1½ cups) water and coconut cream and bring to a boil. Add the fish sauce and reduce the heat. Simmer for 5 minutes, then leave to cool. When the mixture has cooled, add the garlic, shallot, soy sauce and lime juice, spring onion and carrot strips; crumble in the dried chilies.

Stir the sauce and check the consistency – if it is too thick, add a little more water.

To make the rice cakes, steam the rice. Trim and finely chop the spring onions. When the rice is steamed, combine it with the spring onions, rice flour, coconut cream, green peppercorns and 200 ml (1 cup) water. Season with salt.

In a rice cake pan or a nonstick frying pan, heat the peanut oil over a medium heat. Shape small patties with your hands, add to the pan in batches and fry for 5 minutes on each side. Take out and drain on kitchen paper.

Serve the rice cakes hot or cold with the Khmer rice cake dressing.

SONG SAA LUNCH

SONG SAA LUNCH

WATERMELON SALAD

INGREDIENTS / serves 4

1 kg (2¼ lbs) watermelon

12 mint leaves

6 sprigs Thai basil

300 ml (1¼ cup) yoghurt

salt

juice of ½ lime

For the toasted nut and seed mix

30 g (¼ cup) cashew nuts

30 g (¼ cup) almonds

30 g (¼ cup) pistachio nuts

10 g (1 tbsp) white sesame seeds

20 g (⅛ cup) pumpkin seeds

20 g (⅛ cup) sunflower seeds

10 g (1 tbsp) black sesame seeds

METHOD

To make the nut and seed mix, roughly chop the cashew nuts, almonds and pistachio nuts. Put the nuts and the pumpkin, sunflower and sesame seeds into a nonstick frying pan and dry-roast them over medium-low heat for about 8 minutes, being careful not to burn them.

Peel the watermelon and cut the flesh into 2 cm (¾ in) triangles. Chop the mint leaves and the Thai basil.

Season the yoghurt with salt, then stir in the lime juice and the chopped herbs.

Stir the watermelon pieces into the yoghurt mixture, top with the nut and seed mix and serve.

COURGETTE AND CUCUMBER SALAD

INGREDIENTS / serves 4

200 g (1 cup) courgette

200 g (1 cup) cucumber

70 g (⅓ cup) cashew nuts

15 fresh mint leaves

salt and pepper

juice of 1 lime

TO GARNISH

2 tbsp cashew nuts, roasted and crushed

METHOD

Clean and slice the courgette and the cucumber with a Japanese mandolin slicer or other vegetable slicer.

Preheat the oven to 170°C (325°F) and toast the cashew nuts on a baking tray gently for around 8 minutes. Take the nuts out of the oven and let them cool, then chop each one into roughly 3 pieces.

In a bowl, combine the courgette, cucumber and cashew nuts. Tear the mint leaves into small pieces and add. Season with salt and pepper and stir in the lime juice. Scatter with the cashew nuts and serve.

SONG SAA LUNCH

SONG SAA LUNCH

CAMBODIAN MANGO SALAD

INGREDIENTS / serves 4

2 green mangoes

½ red pepper

½ yellow pepper

½ green pepper

1 carrot

2 tomatoes

2 tbsp basil leaves

2 tbsp mint leaves

For the dressing

1 tbsp garlic

1½ tbsp shallots

2 tbsp fresh coriander

1 bird's eye chili

2 tbsp palm sugar

5 tbsp fish sauce

3 tbsp sweet chili sauce

5 tbsp freshly squeezed lime juice

1 tsp salt

TO GARNISH

2 tbsp peanuts, roasted and crushed

METHOD

Peel the green mangoes and cut out the stones. Deseed the red, yellow and green pepper halves. Peel the carrot. Cut the mangoes, peppers and carrot into julienne strips and set aside.

Halve the tomatoes, spoon out the seeds and cut the flesh into slices. Chop the basil and the mint. Combine everything in a salad bowl, then tip it into a colander to drain while preparing the dressing.

To make the dressing, peel and finely chop the garlic and the shallots; chop the coriander and the chili. Put into a small bowl and add the palm sugar, fish sauce, sweet chili sauce, lime juice, salt and 3 tablespoons hot water. Stir well until the sugar has dissolved.

Return the drained salad ingredients to the bowl, pour over the dressing and toss to combine well. Sprinkle with the crushed roasted peanuts and serve.

Tip – You could add green papaya, banana blossom or pomelos to this salad. This salad also tastes delicious if you add some cubed roasted chicken breast fillets or prawns.

SOFT-SHELL CRAB TEMPURA

INGREDIENTS / serves 4

For the crabs

8 soft-shell crabs

2 l (8 cups) peanut oil

24 Thai basil leaves

sea salt

For the tempura batter

85 g (⅔ cup) cornflour

85 g (⅔ cup) flour

250 g (2 cups) fizzy soft drink or beer

For the chili lime caramel

250 g (1 cup) sugar

1 tsp chili flakes

1 lime leaf

METHOD

To make the tempura batter, combine the cornflour, flour and soft drink or beer and leave to stand while you prepare the rest.

Clean and quarter or halve the soft-shell crabs, depending on their size. Pat them dry with a paper towel.

To make the chili lime caramel, put 250 ml (1 cup) water into a small saucepan. Add the sugar, chili flakes and lime leaf and heat over medium heat. Reduce the heat and simmer for about 5 minutes, stirring frequently, until the sugar has dissolved. Increase the heat to medium-high and cook for another 4–5 minutes without stirring until the mixture is a deep golden colour. Leave to cool slightly in the saucepan, then transfer to a container.

Pour the peanut oil into a saucepan, making sure that the oil doesn't take up more than half the volume of the pot. Heat the oil to 165°C (325°F) (small bubbles should appear at the surface).

Add 12 Thai basil leaves and deep-fry for 1 minute. Remove and place on a paper towel to absorb the excess oil.

Now dip the crab pieces into the tempura batter, gently shaking off any excess before placing them into the hot oil. Cook for about 12 minutes until light brown and crisp. Remove and place on paper towels to absorb the excess oil. Season with sea salt while still hot and serve immediately with the deep-fried and fresh basil leaves and the chili lime caramel.

Tip – You can make squid tempura using the same steps. Squid tempura tastes particularly delicious with wasabi mayonnaise. Stir together 80 ml (⅓ cup) mayonnaise and ½ tsp wasabi and serve with the squid.

SONG SAA LUNCH

SONG SAA LUNCH

SCALLOP CEVICHE

INGREDIENTS / serves 4

500 g (1 lb) scallops

1 shallot

½ garlic clove

1 lime leaf

1 bird's eye chili

1–2 tsp fish sauce

100 ml (⅓ cup) lime juice

400 ml (1½ cups) coconut milk

salt

TO GARNISH

5 mint leaves

5 sprigs coriander

5 basil leaves

METHOD

Halve each scallop horizontally.

Peel and very thinly slice the shallot and the garlic, and thinly slice the lime leaf and the chili.

Place the scallops into a bowl with the shallot, garlic, lime leaf and chili, then add the fish sauce, lime juice and coconut milk and stir to combine. Marinate for 2 hours in the fridge.

Just before serving, check the seasoning and add salt or more fish sauce. Divide between four plates. Chop the mint, coriander and basil leaves, sprinkle over the plates and serve.

KAMPOT PEPPER SQUID

INGREDIENTS / serves 4

600 g (1 lb 5 oz) squid, cleaned

20 g (⅛ cup) garlic

100 g (½ cup) onion

100 g (½ cup) green pepper, sliced (optional)

100 g (½ cup) red pepper, sliced (optional)

50 ml (4 tbsp) cooking oil

100 g (½ cup) green Kampot peppercorns

10 ml (2 tsp) fish sauce

45 ml (3 tbsp) oyster sauce

30 ml (2 tbsp) soy sauce

10 ml (2 tsp) sesame oil

5 g (1 tsp) palm sugar

2 tbsp stock (or water)

TO GARNISH

100 g (½ cup) chopped spring onions

METHOD

Wash the squid under cold running water, remove the skins and cut them into triangles. Peel and chop the garlic and the onion. If liked, slice a green and a red pepper.

Bring a wok to a medium to high heat, add the cooking oil, garlic, onion, green pepper, red pepper and Kampot peppercorns. Stir-fry for 1 minute. Add the squid and stir-fry for another 2 minutes. Add the fish sauce, oyster sauce, soy sauce, sesame oil, palm sugar and 2 tablespoons of stock or water. Simmer for 3–4 minutes until the squid is cooked. Check the seasoning.

SONG SAA LUNCH

SONG SAA LUNCH

CRISPY VERMICELLI

INGREDIENTS / serves 4

150 g (5 oz) white cabbage

150 g (5 oz) red cabbage

150 g (5 oz) cucumber

100 g (3½ oz) carrots

200 g (3½ oz) vermicelli

2 litres (8 cups) peanut oil

250 g (9 oz) chicken breast fillets

For the dressing

5 tbsp fish sauce

1 tsp salt

1 tbsp palm sugar

1 tsp chopped garlic

2 tbsp chopped shallots

1 tbsp chopped coriander

1 bird's eye chili, chopped

3 tbsp sweet chili sauce

5 tbsp fresh lime juice

TO GARNISH

5 sprigs Thai basil

5 sprigs mint

20 g (⅛ cup) roasted peanuts

METHOD

Cut the white cabbage, red cabbage, cucumber and carrot into julienne strips. Set aside.

Bring 5 tablespoons water to a boil. Put aside, add the fish sauce, salt and palm sugar and let cool. Add the garlic, shallots, coriander, chili, sweet chili sauce and lime juice.

Vermicelli cook very quickly, so make sure that everything is ready before you start. Line a plate with a paper towel. Cut the vermicelli in half and separate them so they crisp evenly. Pour the peanut oil into a large saucepan and heat it to 80–85°C (175–185°F). When the oil is hot, do a test. Add a small amount of vermicelli to the hot oil and cook for just 2–3 seconds. Immediately remove from the oil. Repeat with the remaining vermicelli. Lift them out and drain them on a plate lined with kitchen paper to absorb the excess oil.

Preheat the oven to 180°C (350°F), season the chicken fillets with salt and roast for about 35 minutes, depending on the thickness of the meat. Check after 25 minutes if the fillets are tender.

Cut the roasted chicken into cubes and combine with the vegetables and the fried vermicelli. Pour over the dressing and toss to combine. Garnish with the Thai basil and mint, and sprinkle with roasted peanuts, then serve.

PAD THAI

INGREDIENTS / serves 4

For the pad thai sauce

1 tbsp tamarind purée

2 tbsp hoisin sauce

3 tbsp oyster sauce

4 tbsp Sriracha chili sauce

4 tbsp sweet soy sauce

3 tbsp fish sauce

1 tbsp salt

For the pad thai noodles

400 g (7 oz) rice noodles

30 g (2 tsp) garlic

30 g (2 tsp) shallots

200 g (1 cup) tofu

100 g (½ cup) aubergine

60 g (¼ cup) cooked shiitake mushrooms

4 tbsp vegetable oil

2 pak choy

100 g (½ cup) beansprouts

100 g (½ cup) mangetouts

1 tbsp Thai curry paste

2 eggs

sugar, to taste

soy sauce, to taste

2 tbsp coconut milk

TO SERVE

2 tbsp peanuts

10 g (2 tsp) shallots

10 g (2 tsp) shredded coconut powder

10 g (2 tsp) fresh coriander

2 bird's eye chilies

2 lime wedges

METHOD

To make the pad thai sauce, stir together all the ingredients and set aside.

Prepare the pad thai noodles. Put the rice noodles in water to soak for 1 hour. Peel and chop the garlic and the shallots. Cut the tofu and the aubergine into cubes. Slice the shiitake mushrooms.

Heat a wok over high heat. Add a little oil, and the rest of the vegetables with the Thai curry paste. Stir-fry for 20 seconds, then crack in the eggs and stir in the drained pad thai noodles, stirring for a few minutes more.

Now add the pad thai sauce, sugar, soy sauce and coconut milk. Stir until the noodles are cooked.

To serve, dry-roast the peanuts in a nonstick frying pan without fat. Peel, chop and deep-fry the shallots. Toast the coconut. Cut the coriander into long, thin strips. Garnish and serve with the roasted peanuts, deep-fried shallots, toasted coconut, coriander strips, chilies and lime wedges.

Tip – Replace the tofu with chicken or shrimps.

SONG SAA LUNCH

SONG SAA LUNCH

DUCK SALAD WITH BLACK SESAME

INGREDIENTS / serves 4

4 duck legs

salt and pepper

2 cucumbers

10 g (2 tsp) black sesame seeds

10 sprigs coriander

10 sprigs Thai basil

10 mint leaves

For the dressing

2 tbsp lime juice

1 tsp tamarind paste

4 tbsp fish sauce

2 tbsp palm sugar

METHOD

Preheat the oven to 200°C (400°F, top and bottom heat).

Clean the duck legs and pat them dry with a paper towel. Season with salt and pepper on both sides. Place the legs in an ovenproof dish and roast in the oven for 45–50 minutes.

Meanwhile, halve the cucumbers lengthways and scrape out the seeds. Using a potato peeler, peel off thin ribbons from the cucumber halves. Place the ribbons in a sieve, add a little salt and leave to drain.

In a hot nonstick frying pan without fat, dry-roast the sesame seeds for a few minutes. Remove and set aside.

To make the dressing, whisk together the lime juice, tamarind paste, fish sauce and palm sugar.

Take the duck legs out of the oven when they are tender and let them cool. Pull the skin and meat off the bone; roughly chop the meat. Chop the coriander, basil and mint.

In a salad bowl, combine the duck meat, cucumber ribbons, sesame seeds and herbs. Pour in the dressing and toss to combine, then serve.

LAMB CUTLETS WITH FRESH SPINACH

INGREDIENTS / serves 4

400 g (13 oz) lamb cutlets

salt

2 tbsp vegetable oil

100 g (3½ oz) fresh spinach

10 sprigs coriander

For the smoked chili dressing

1 long chili

2 garlic cloves

1 tbsp vinegar

6 tbsp quality olive oil

1 tbsp Dijon mustard

TO GARNISH

50 g (¼ cup) toasted cashew nuts

25 g (⅛ cup) toasted sesame seeds

METHOD

Season the lamb cutlets with salt. Heat the vegetable oil in a frying pan over a high heat. Add the cutlets and fry for 2 minutes on each side. Take the pan off the heat and leave to rest for 5 minutes.

To make the dressing, burn the chili over a flame until it is completely black, then wrap it in cling film and leave to sweat for 10 minutes. Remove the cling film and rinse off the blackened skin – it should come off easily. Halve and deseed the chili. Peel the garlic. Very finely chop the chili and the garlic. Place the chili, garlic, vinegar, olive oil and mustard into a bowl and whisk together until emulsified.

Preheat the oven to 180°C (350°F). Spread the cashew nuts and sesame seeds in a single layer on a baking tray and cook in the oven for about 8–12 minutes. Roughly chop the nuts and combine with the seed.

Clean and trim the spinach and chop the coriander, then add both to the bowl. Toss with the dressing to combine. Top with the lamb cutlets and garnish with the nut and seed mixture, then serve.

SONG SAA LUNCH

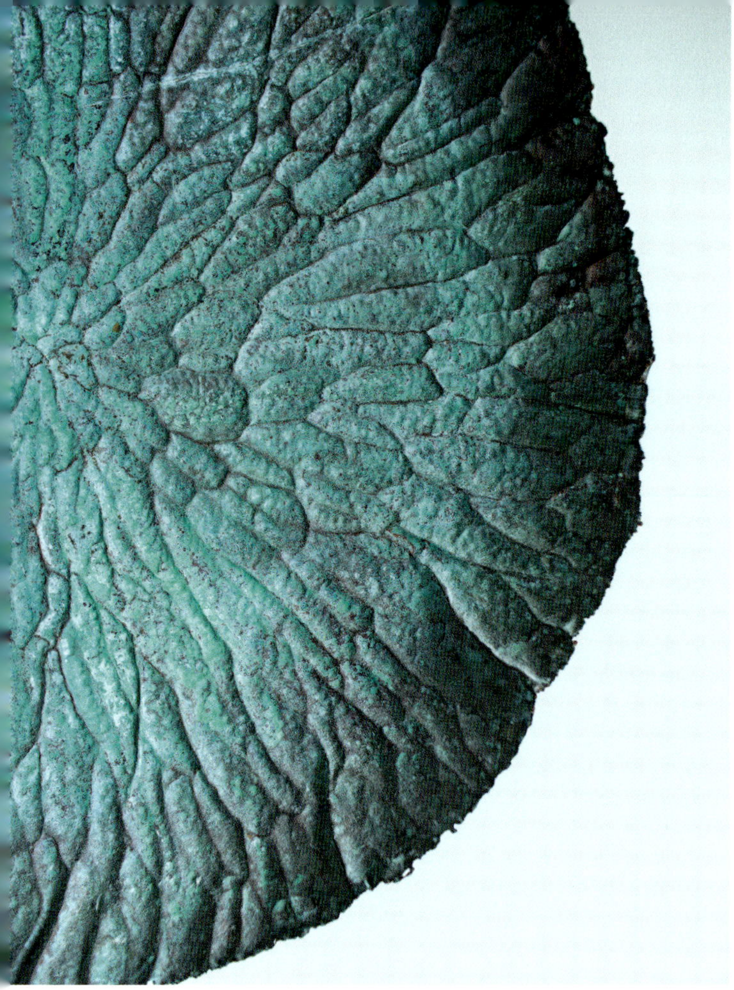

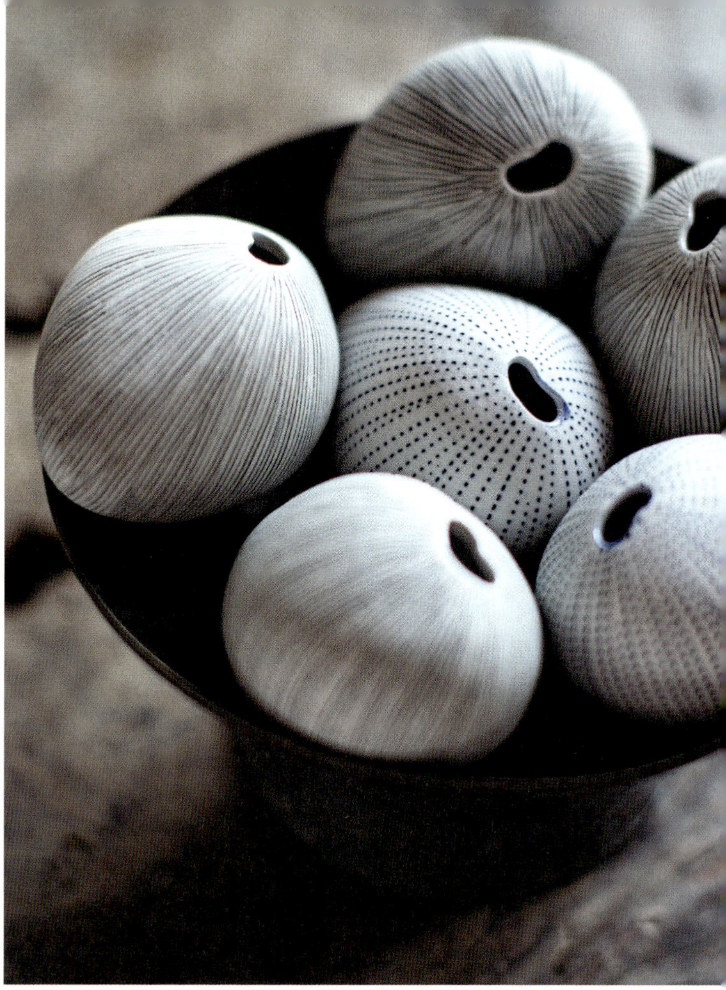

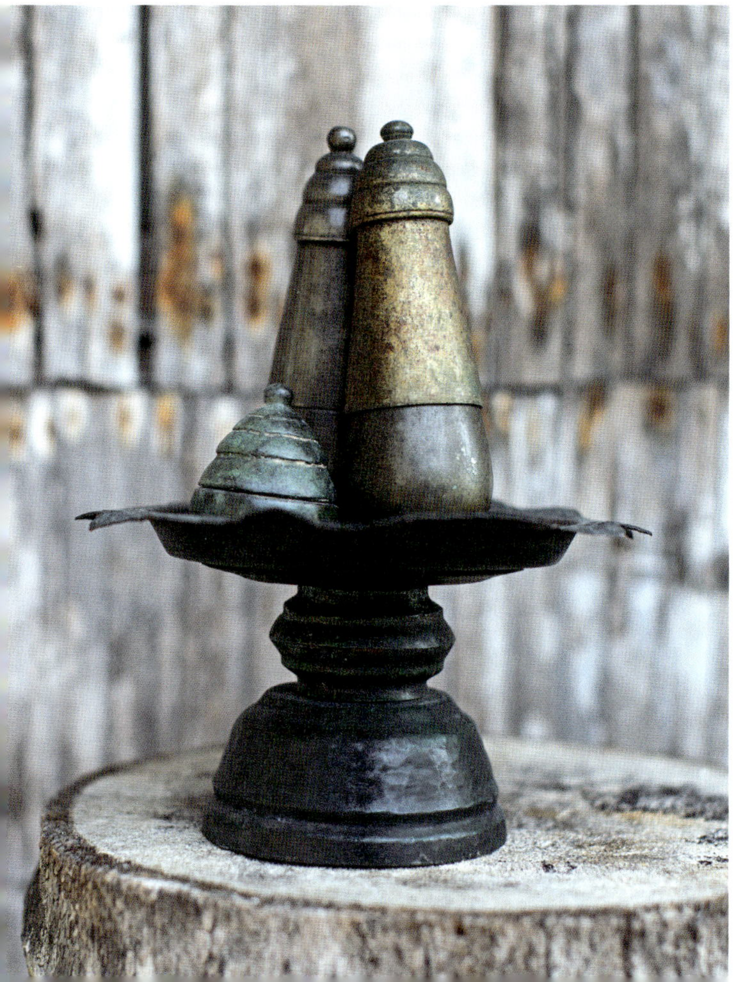

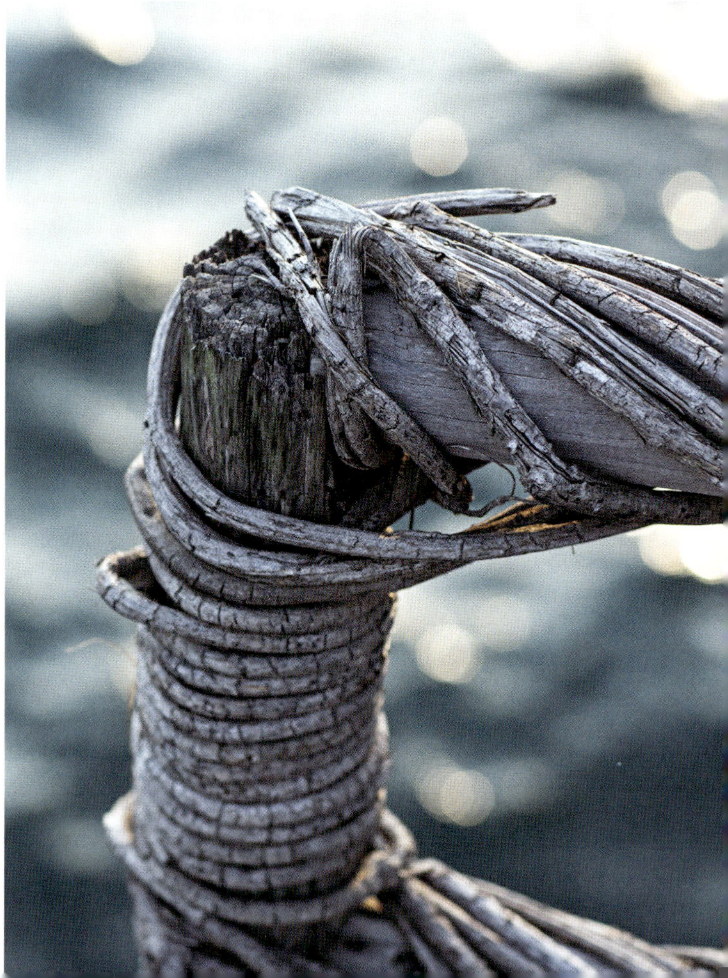

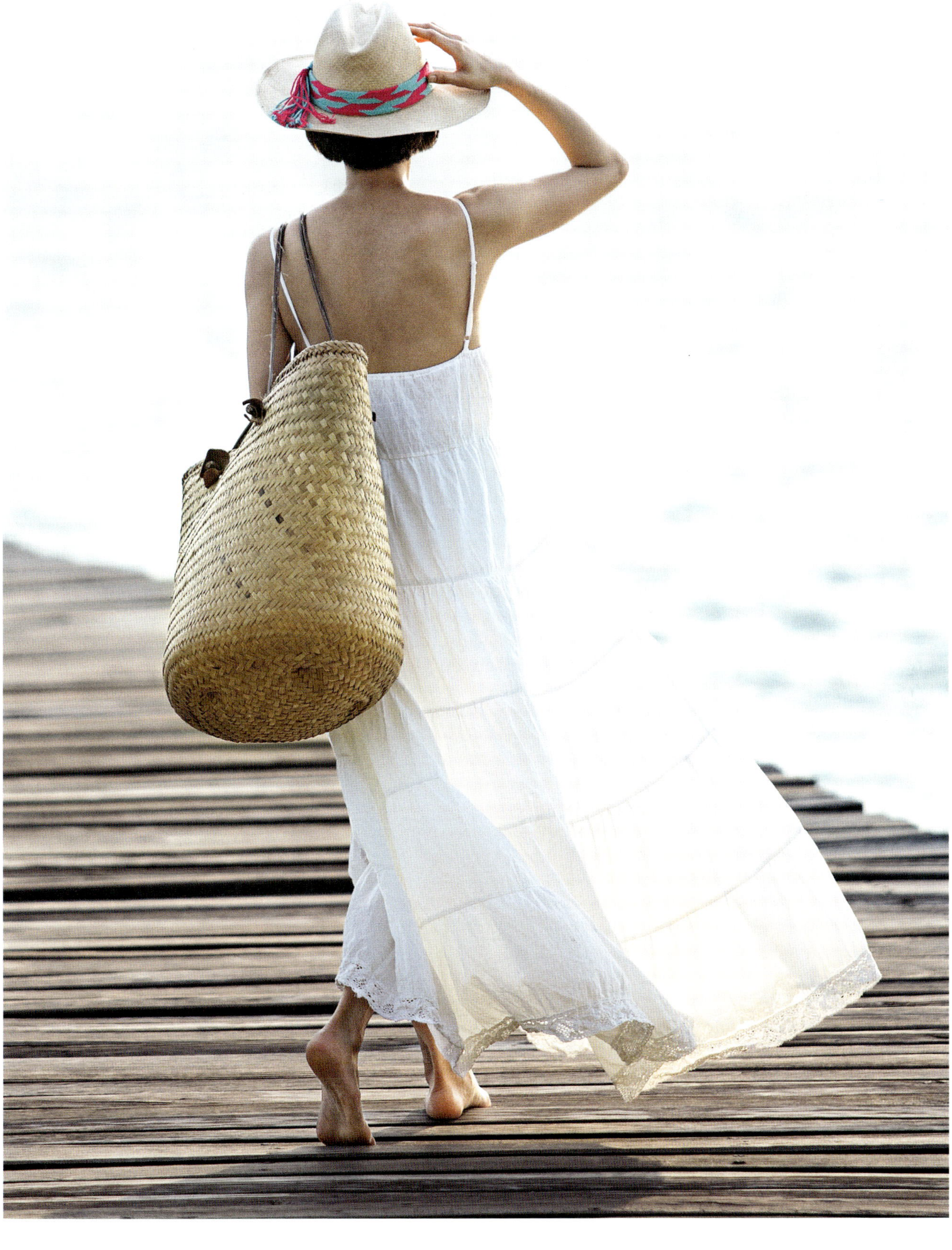

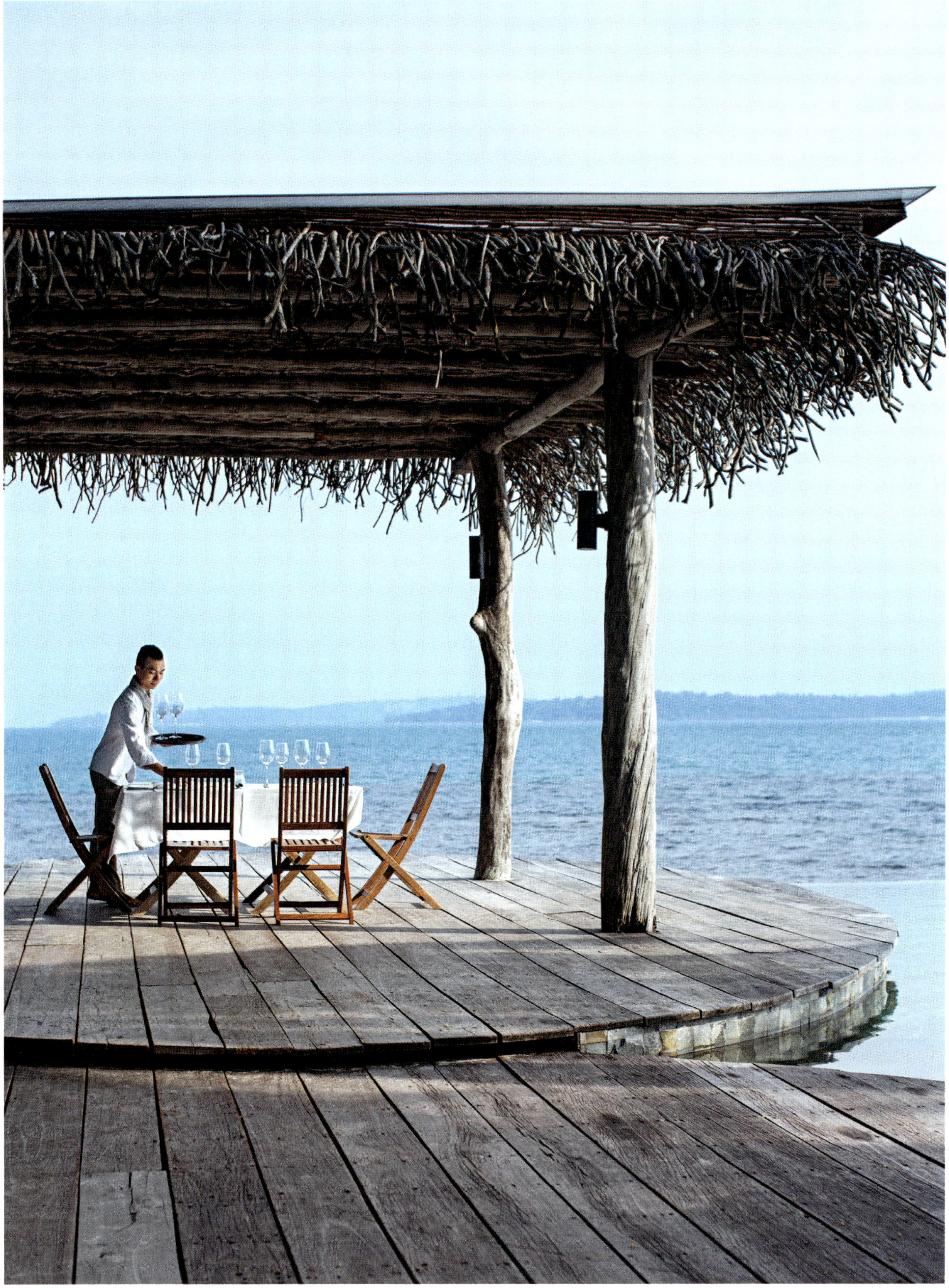

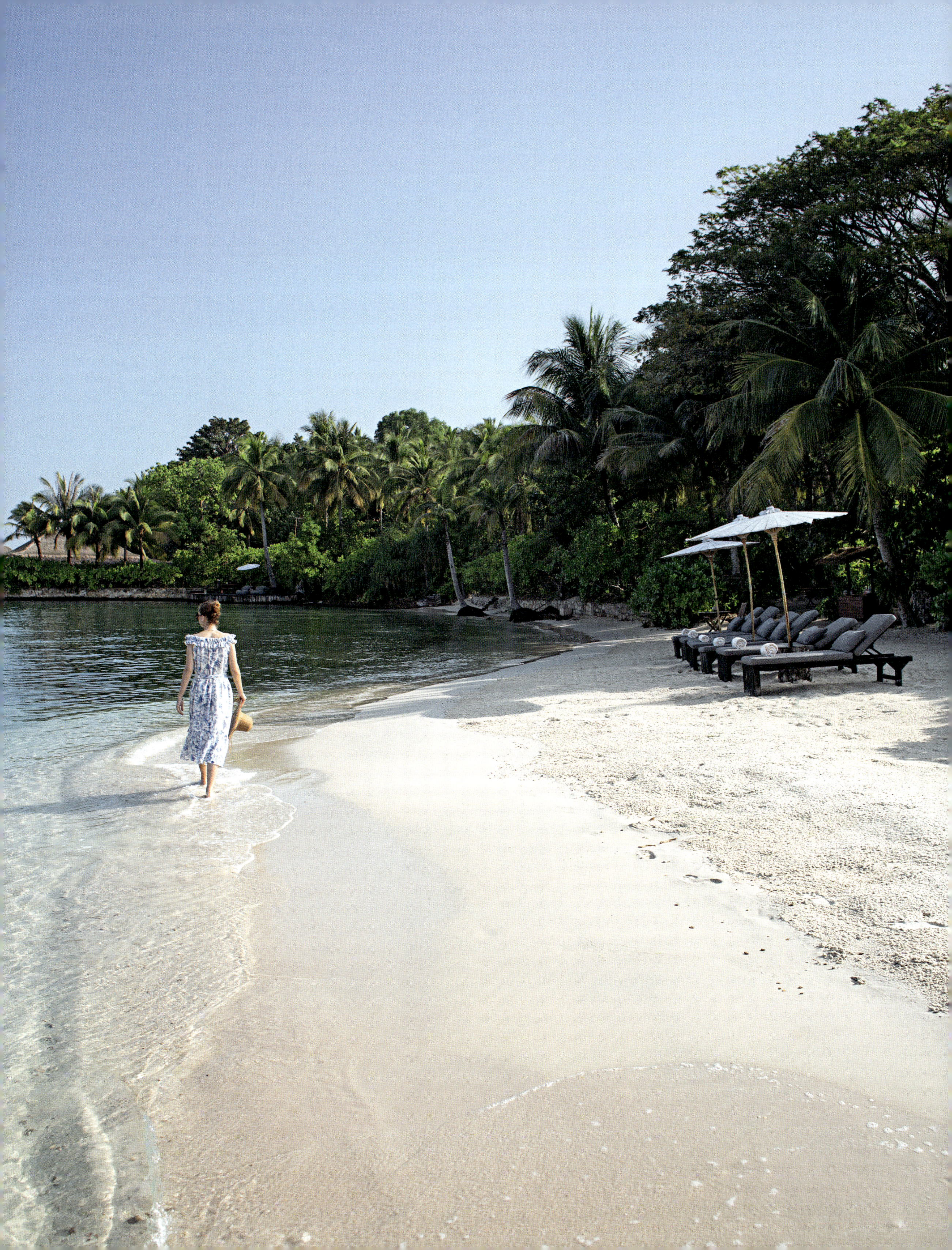

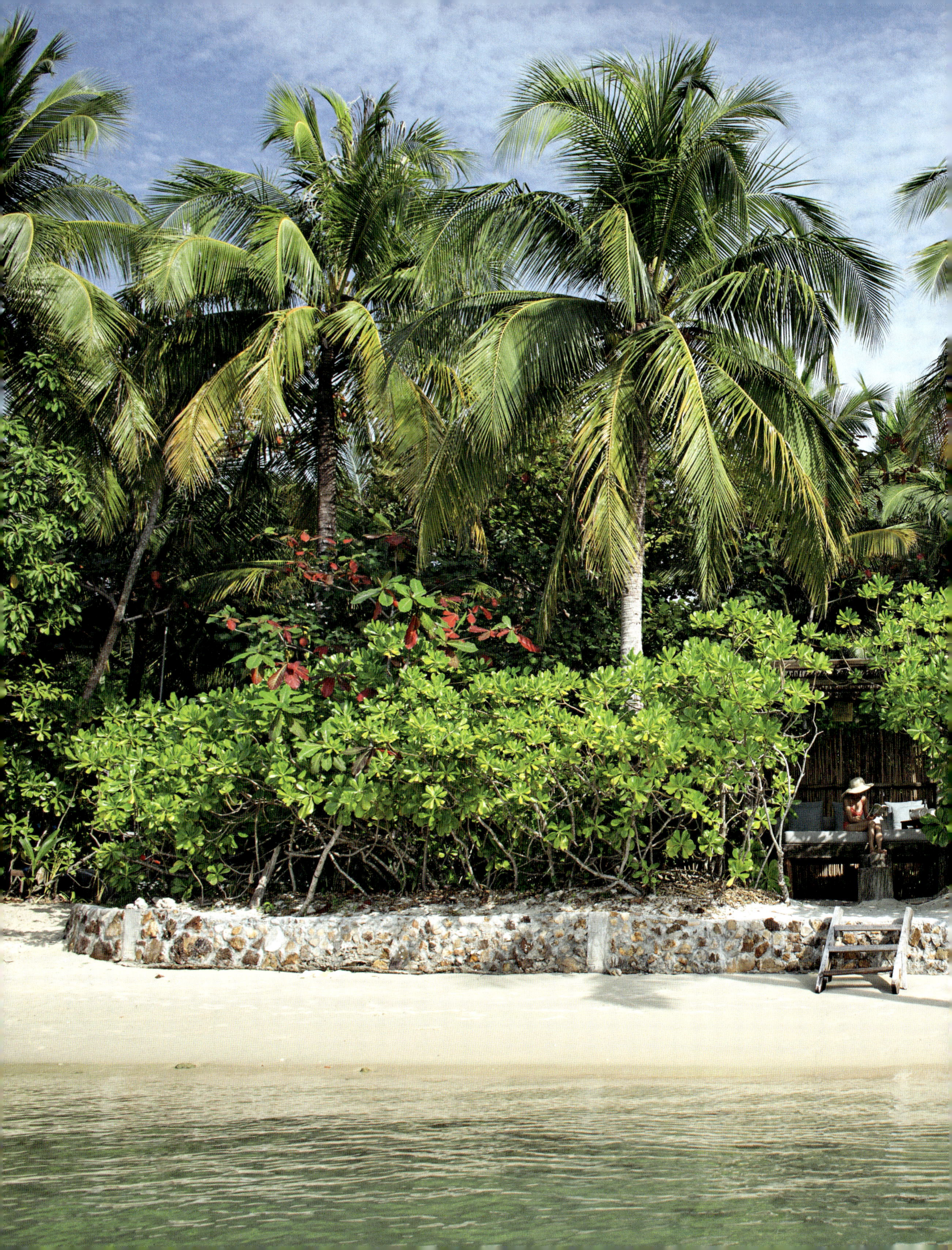

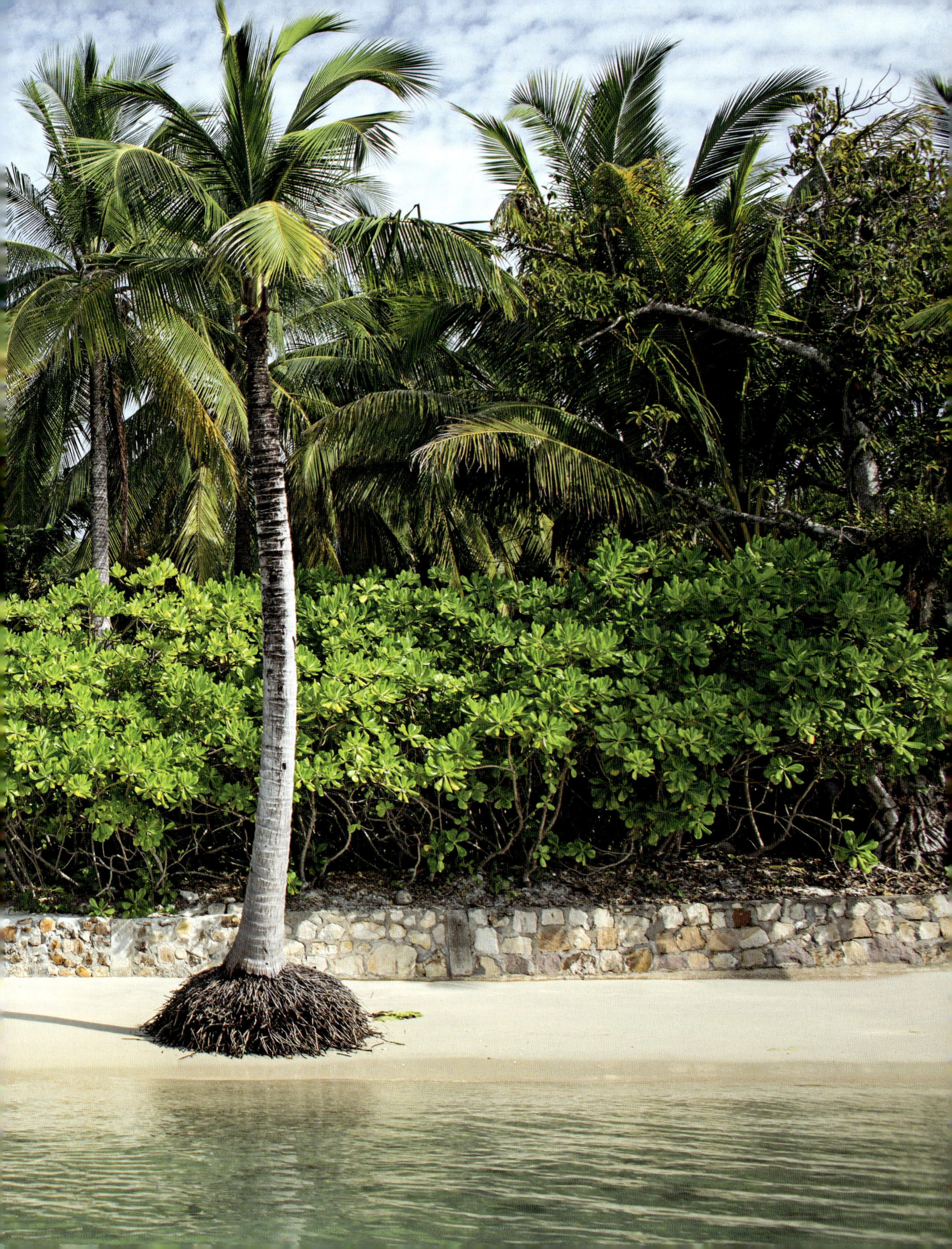

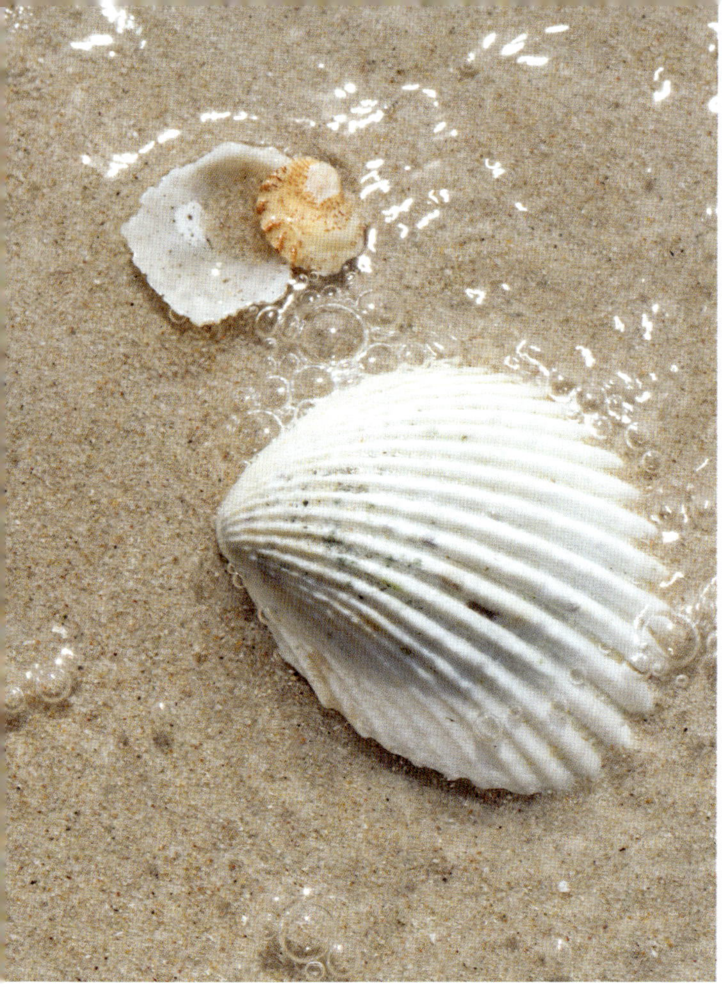
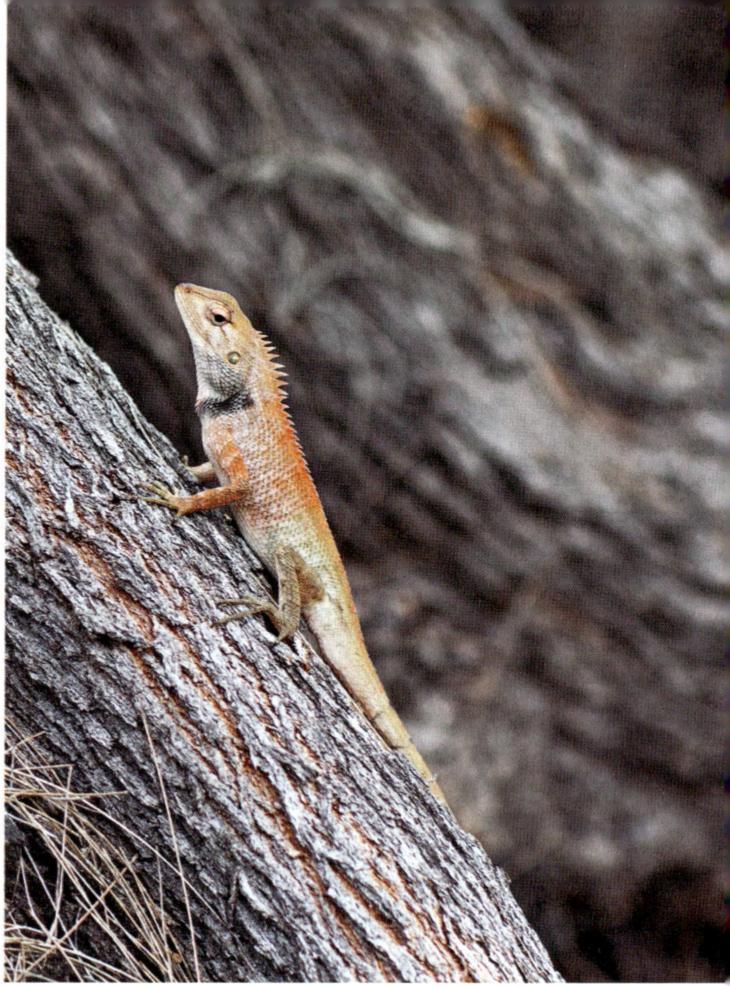
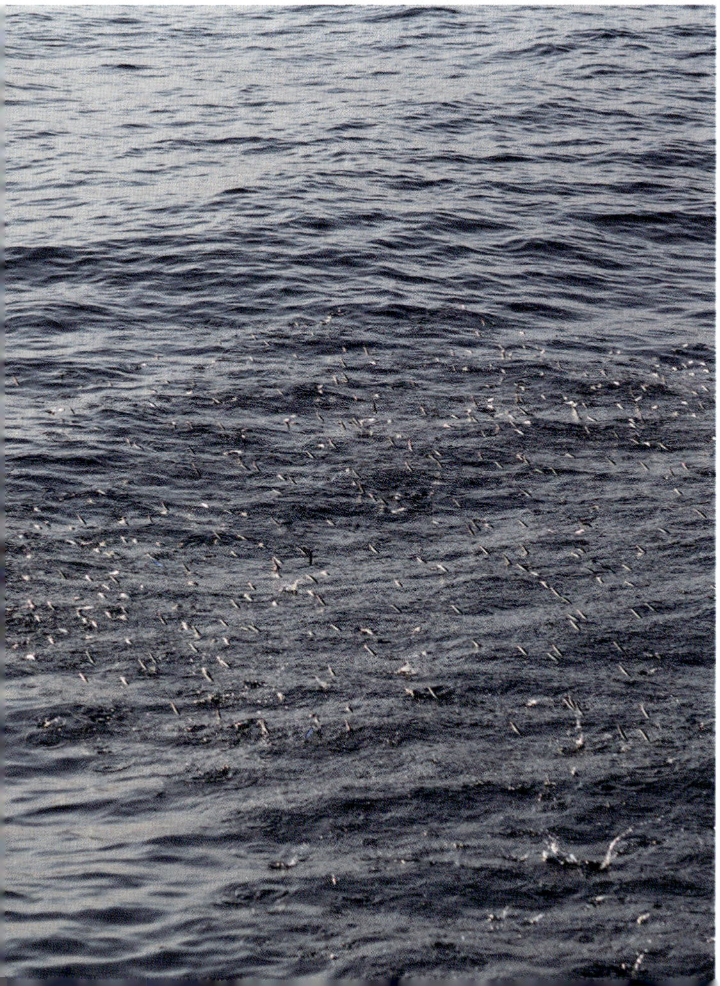
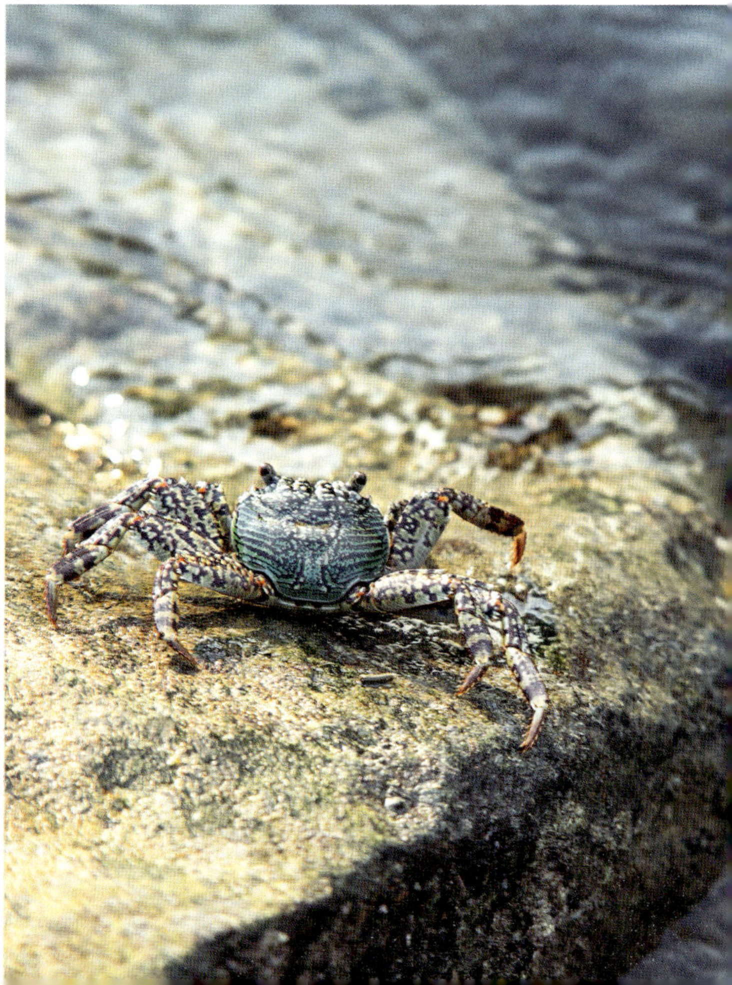

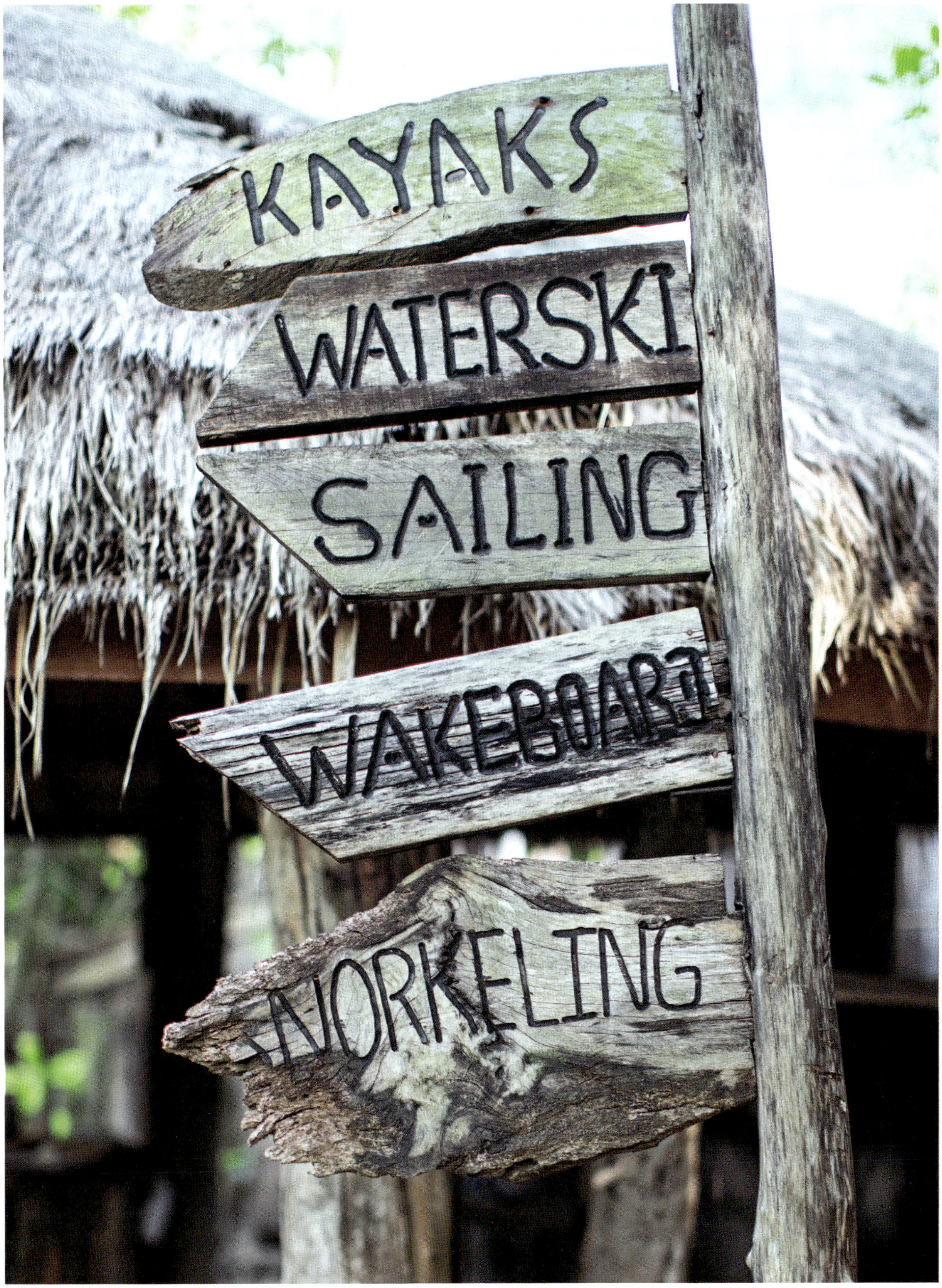
KAYAKS
WATERSKI
SAILING
WAKEBOAR
NORKELING

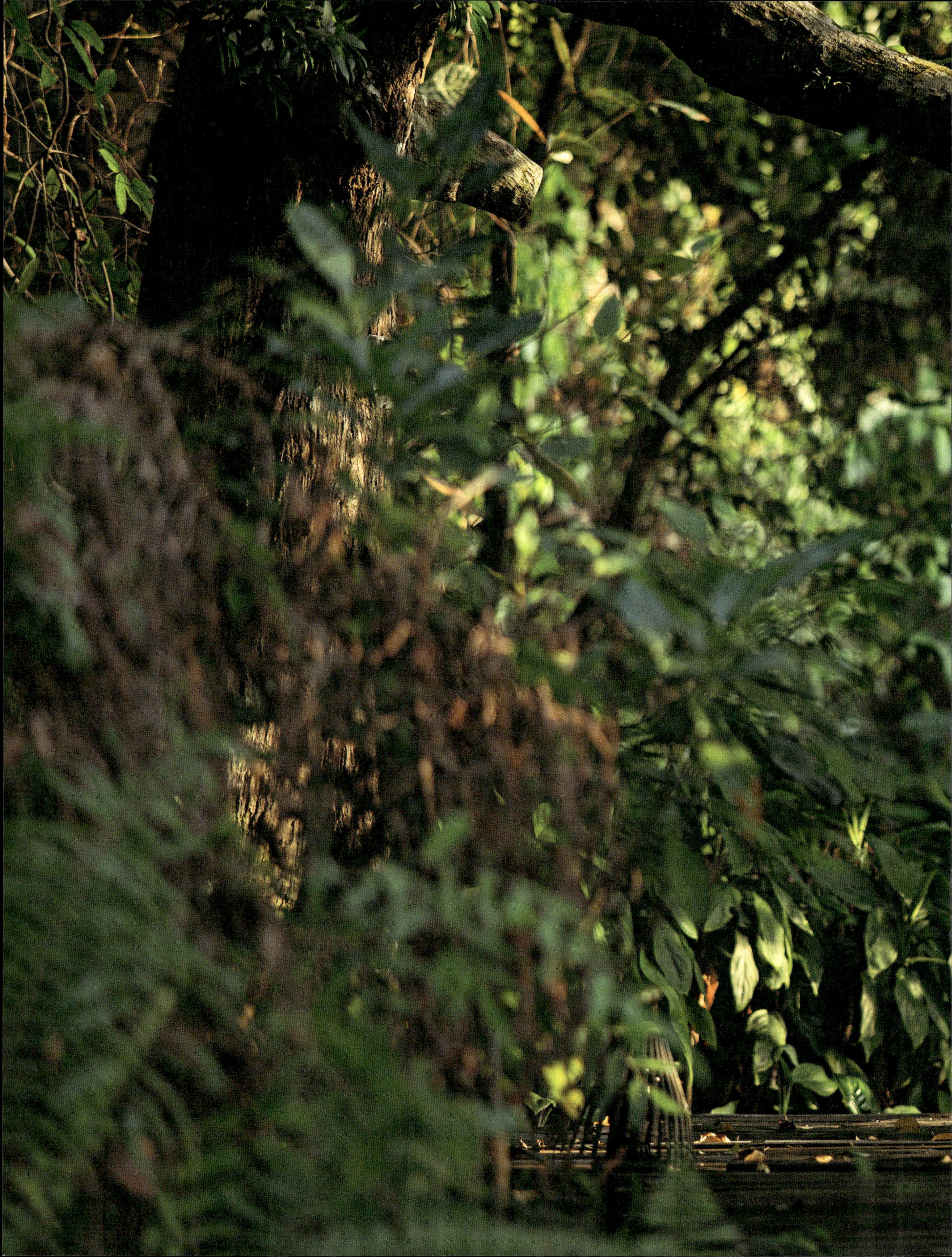

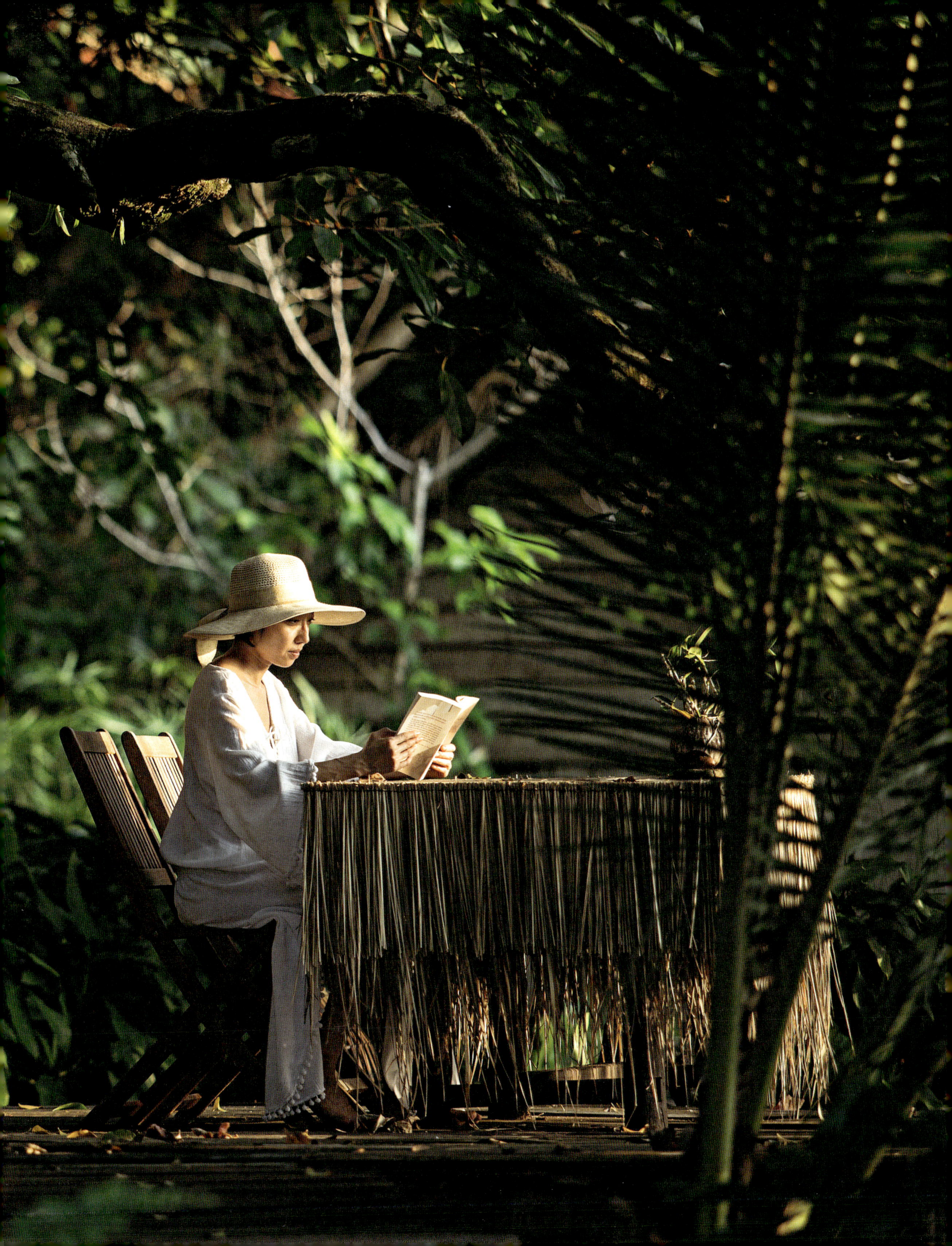

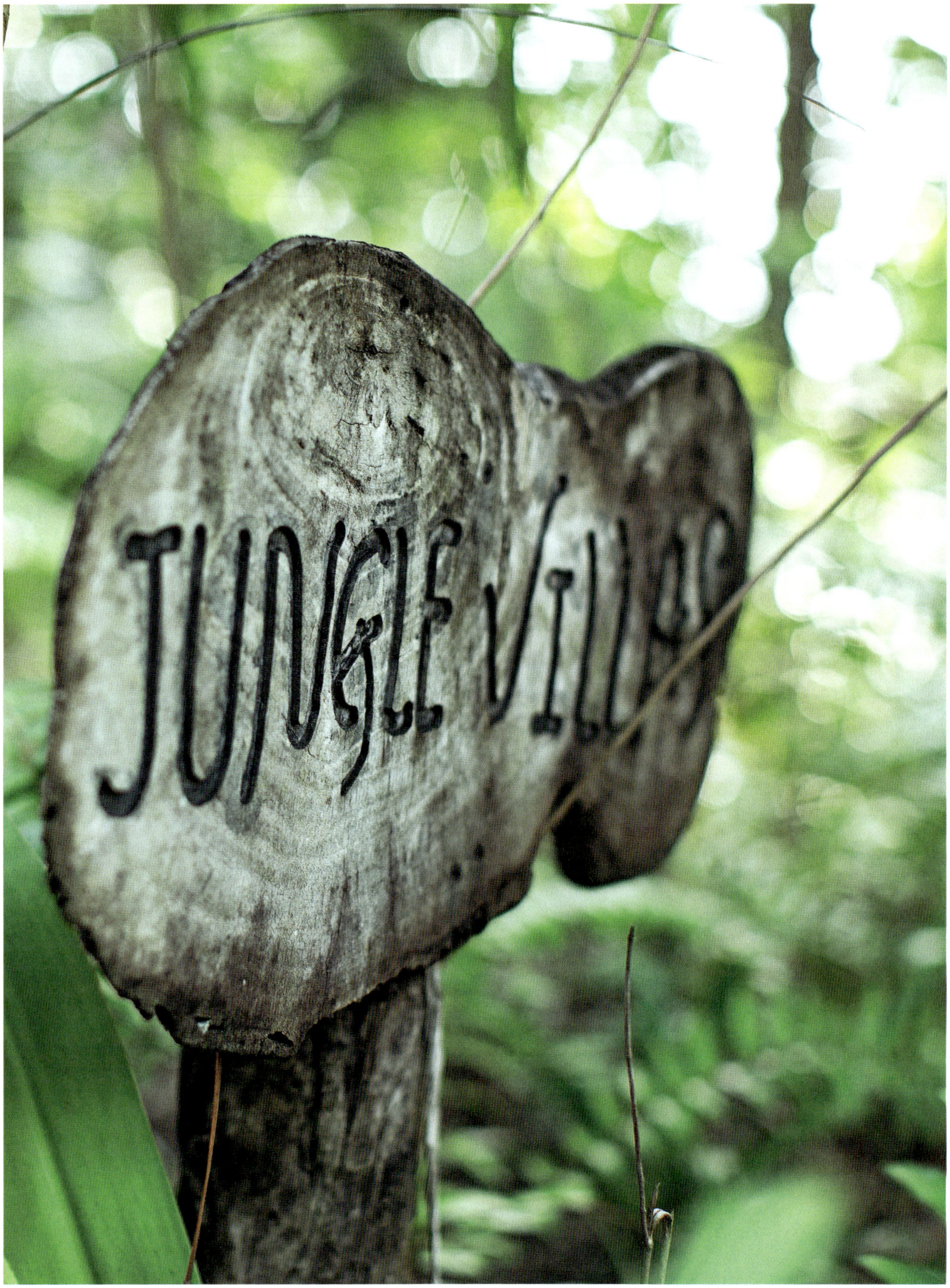
JUNGLE

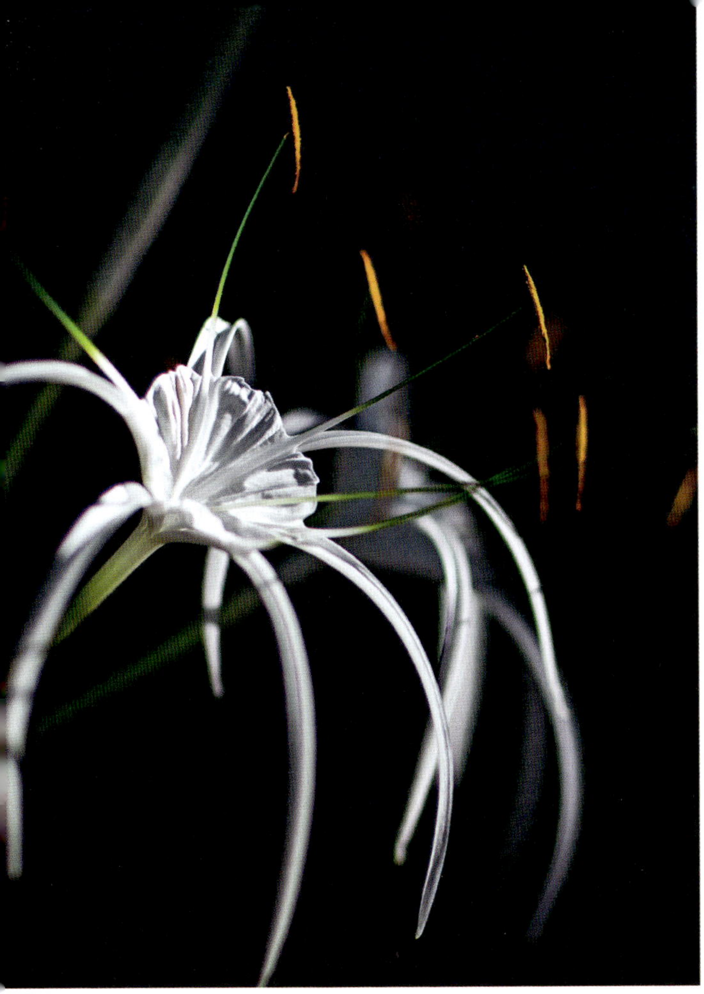
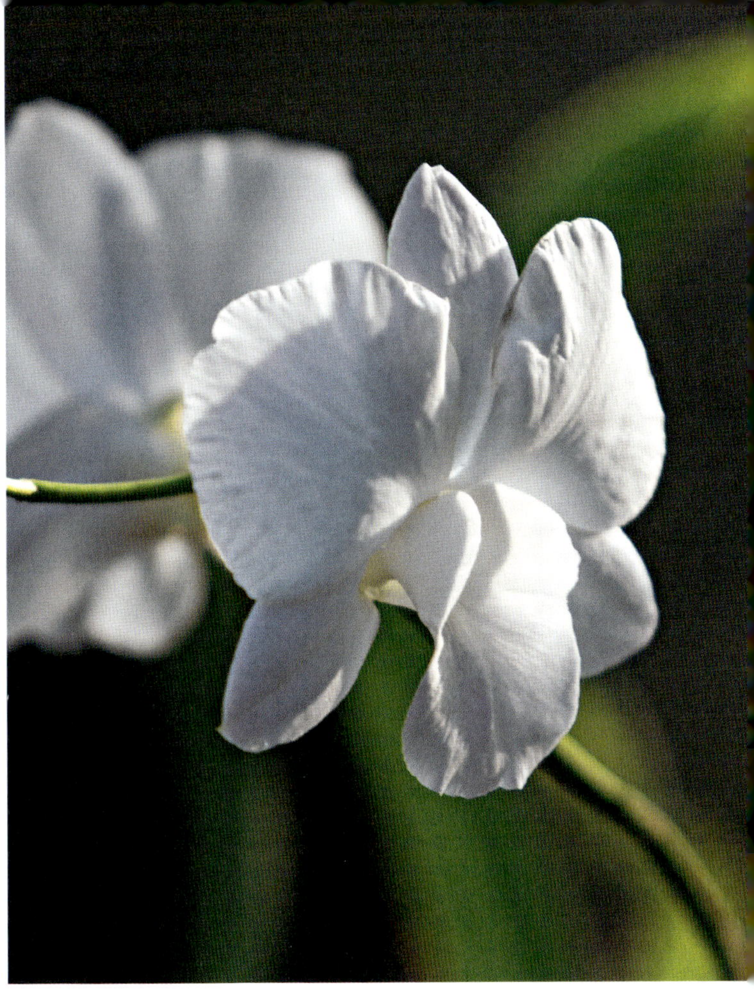
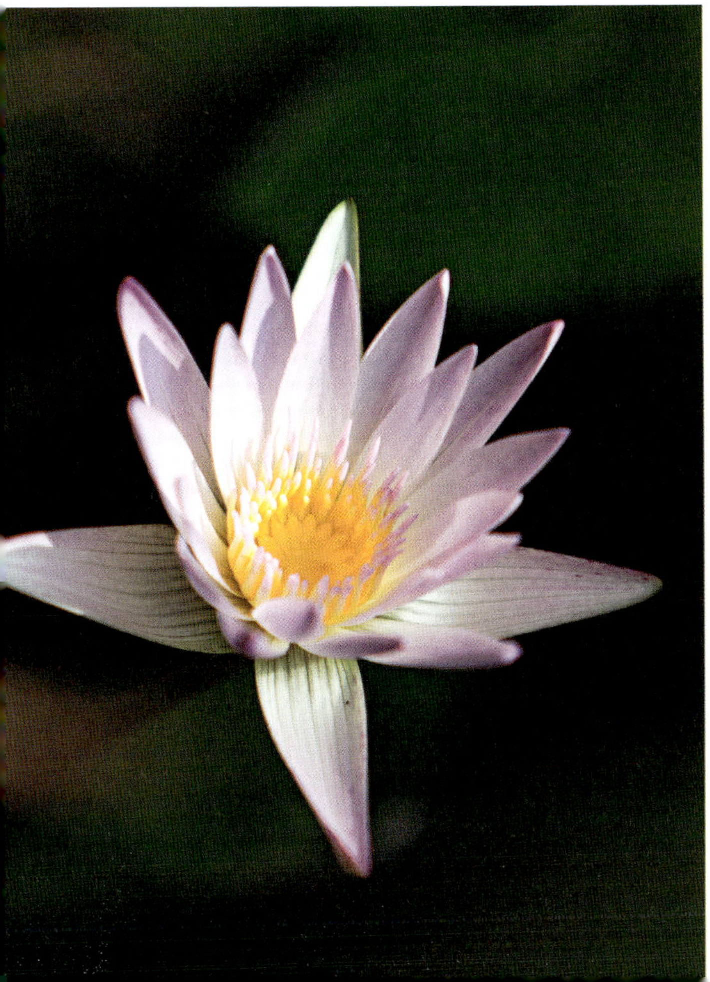
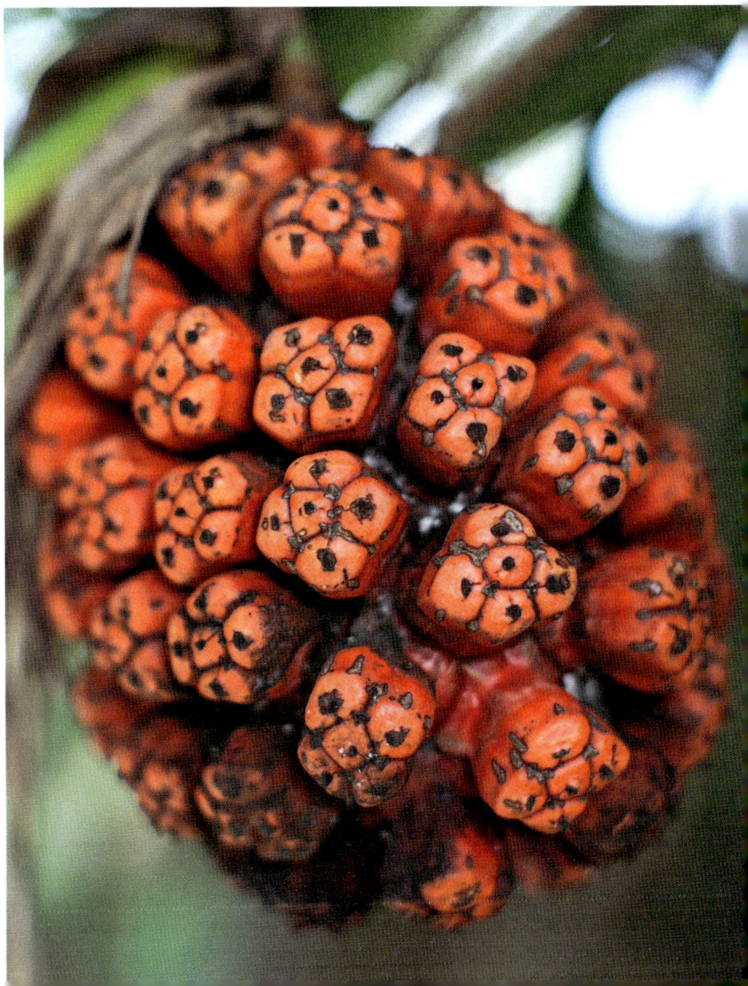

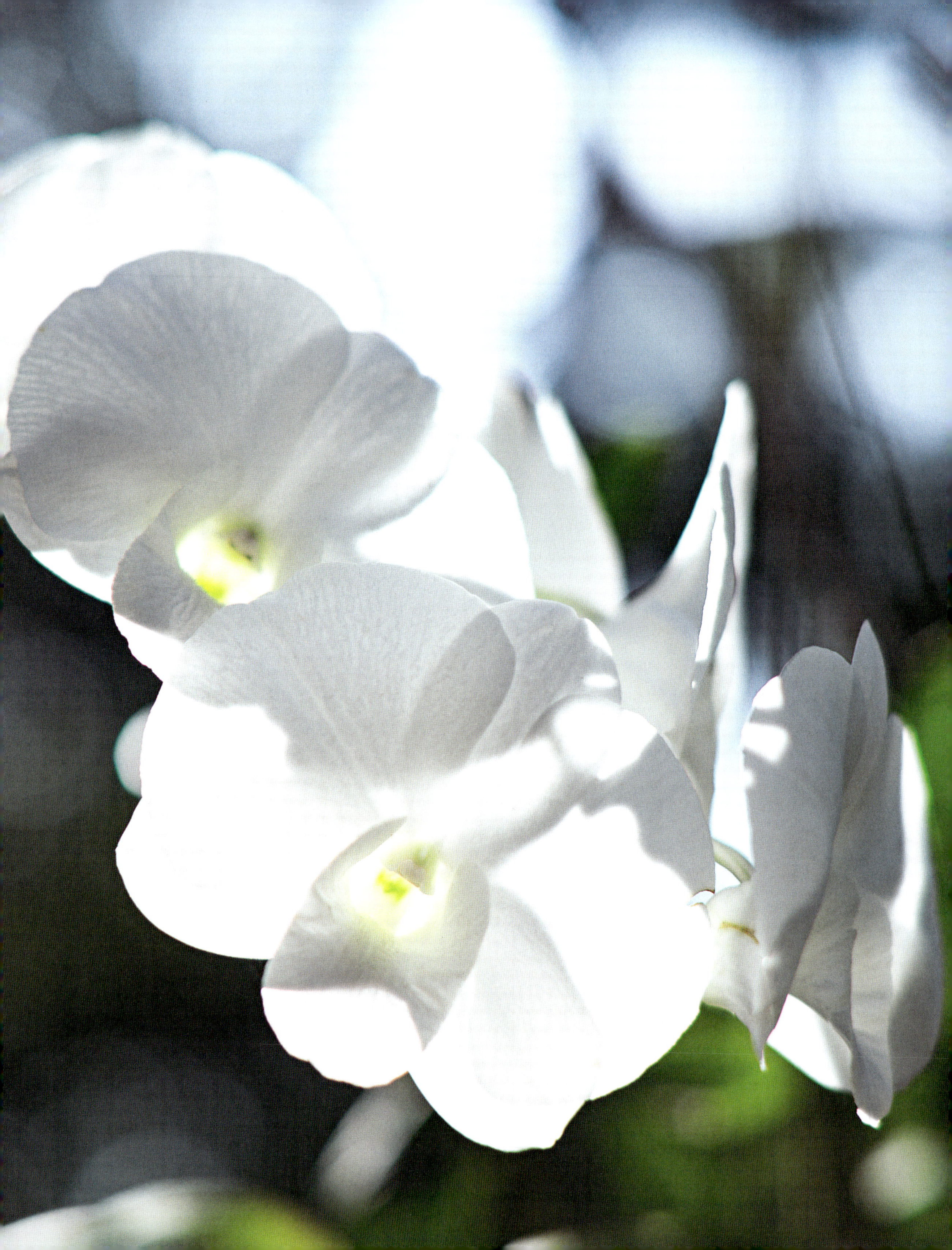

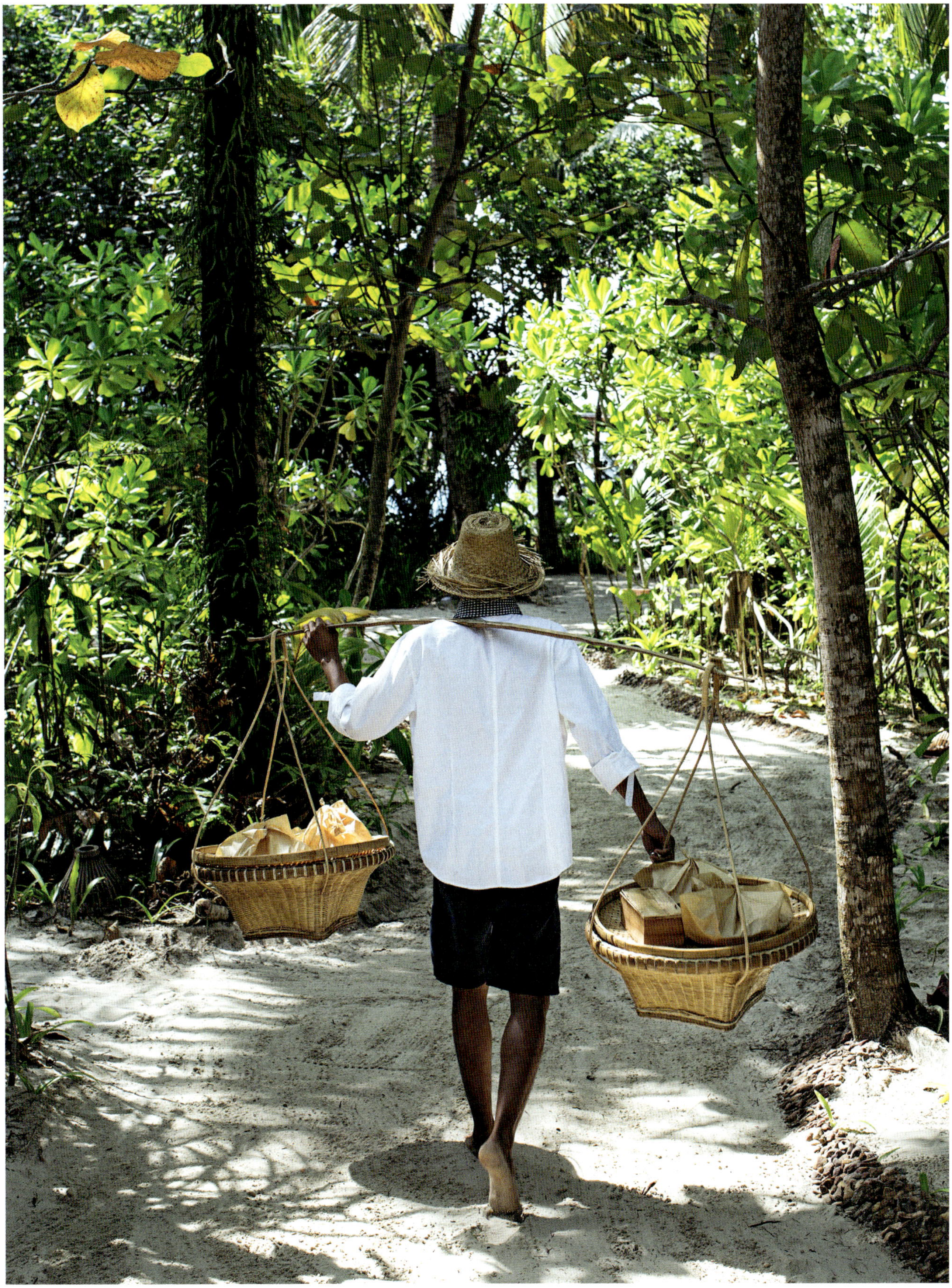

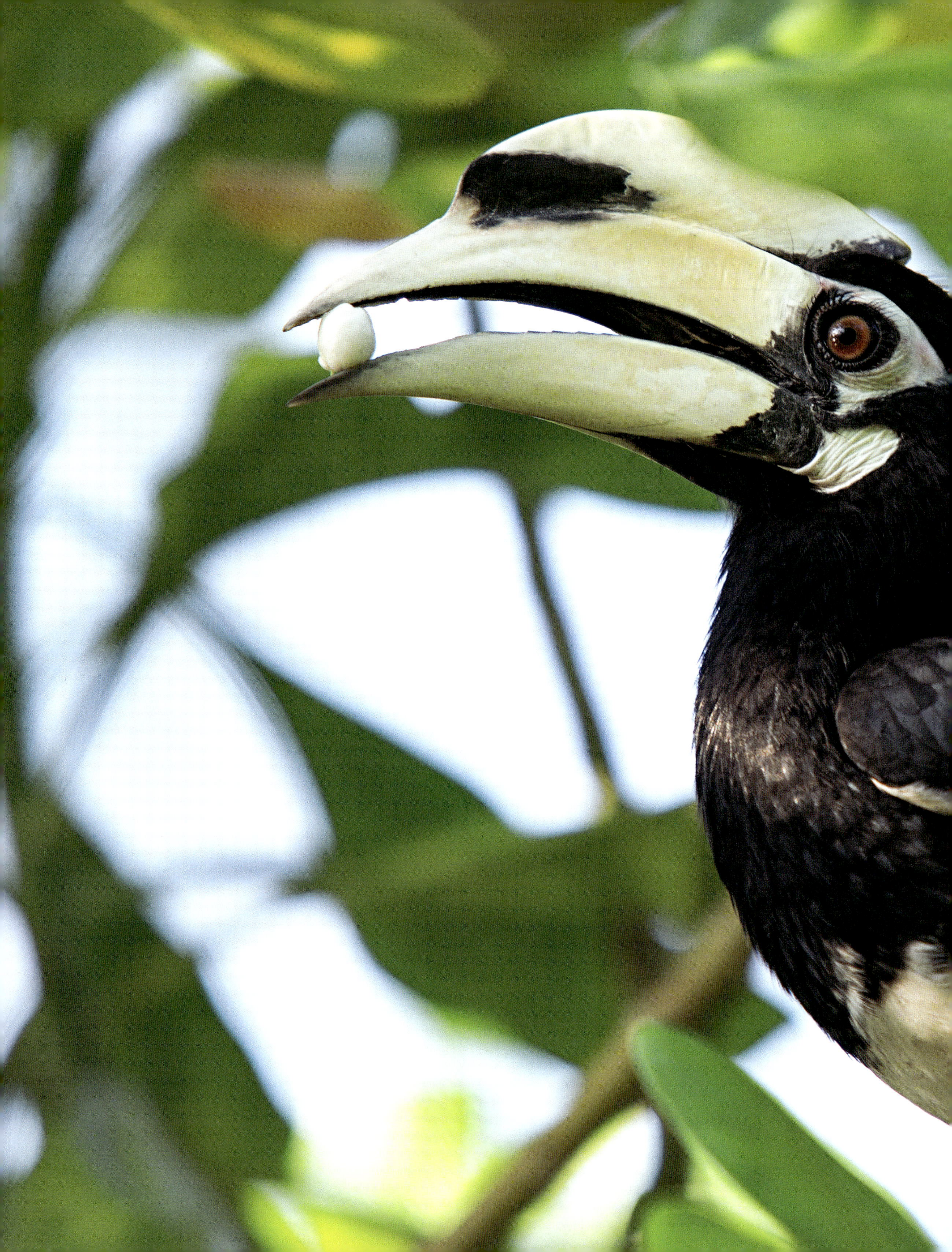

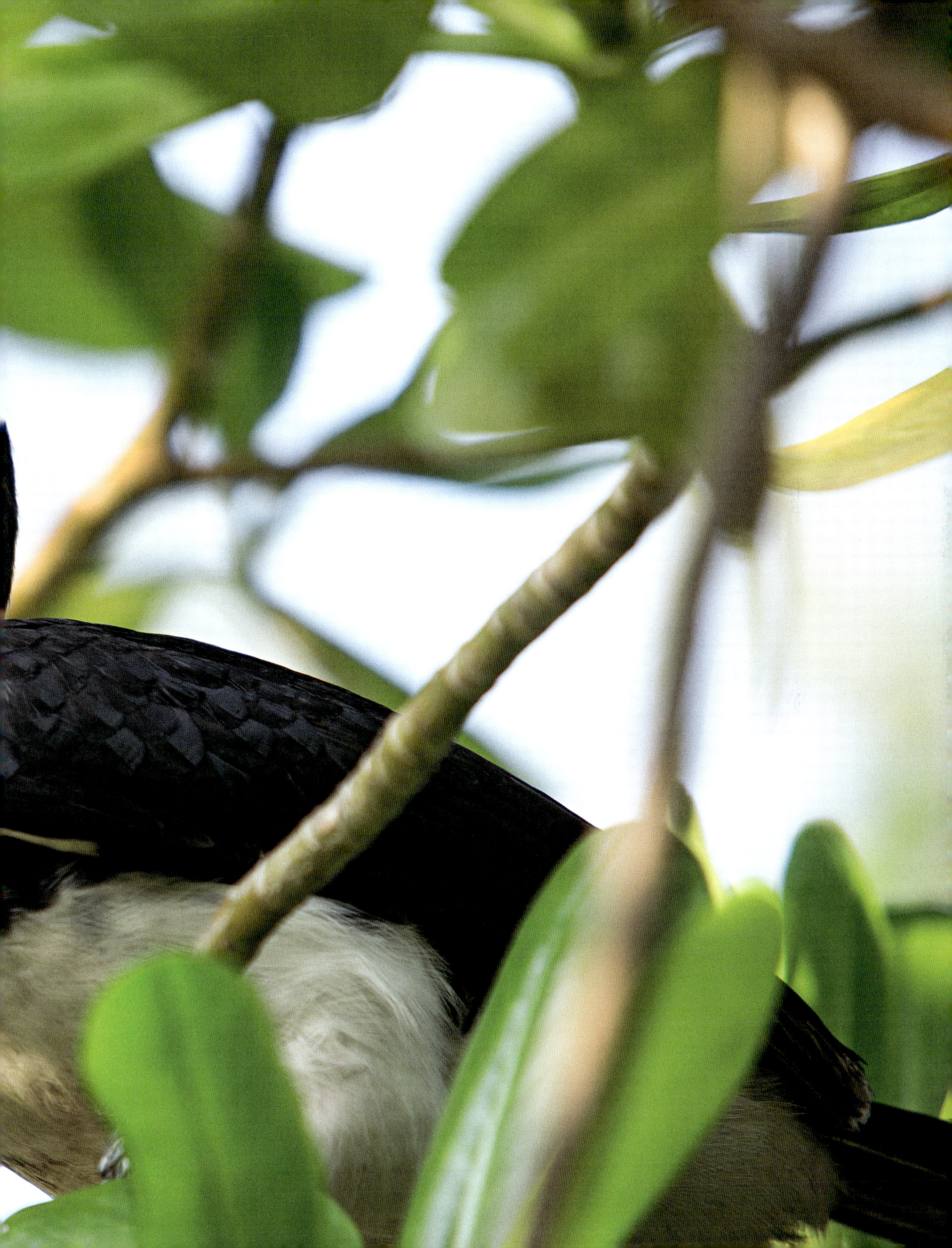

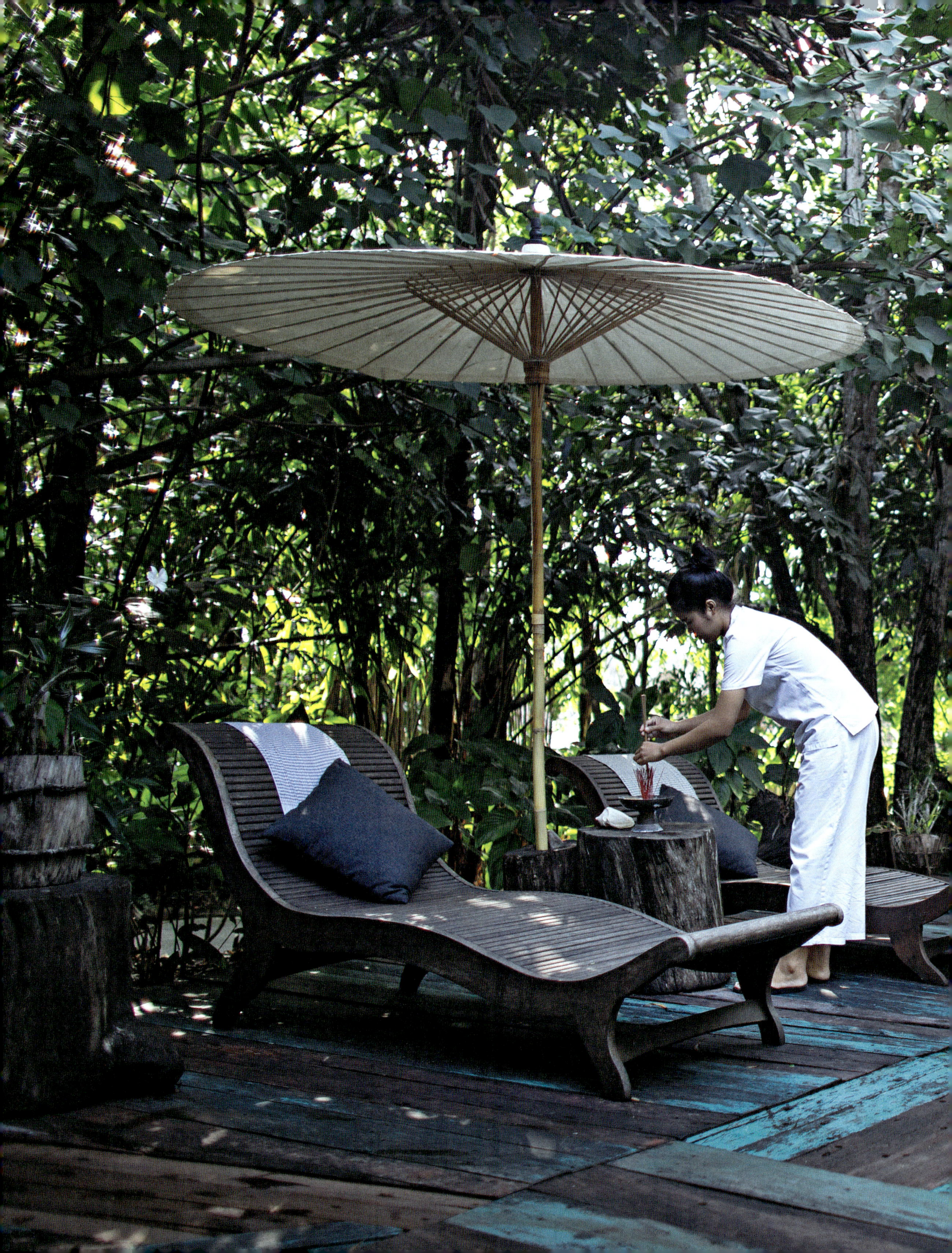

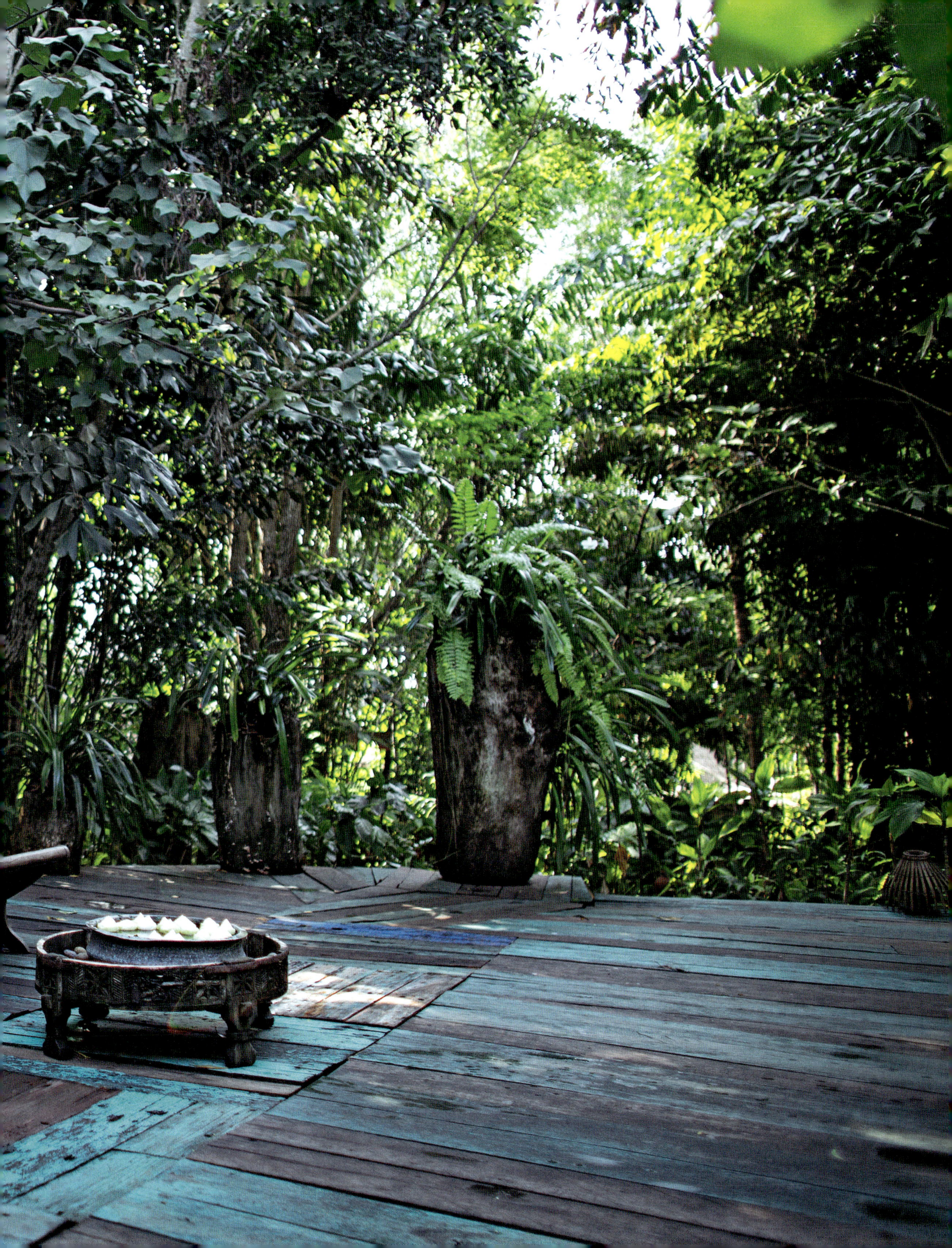

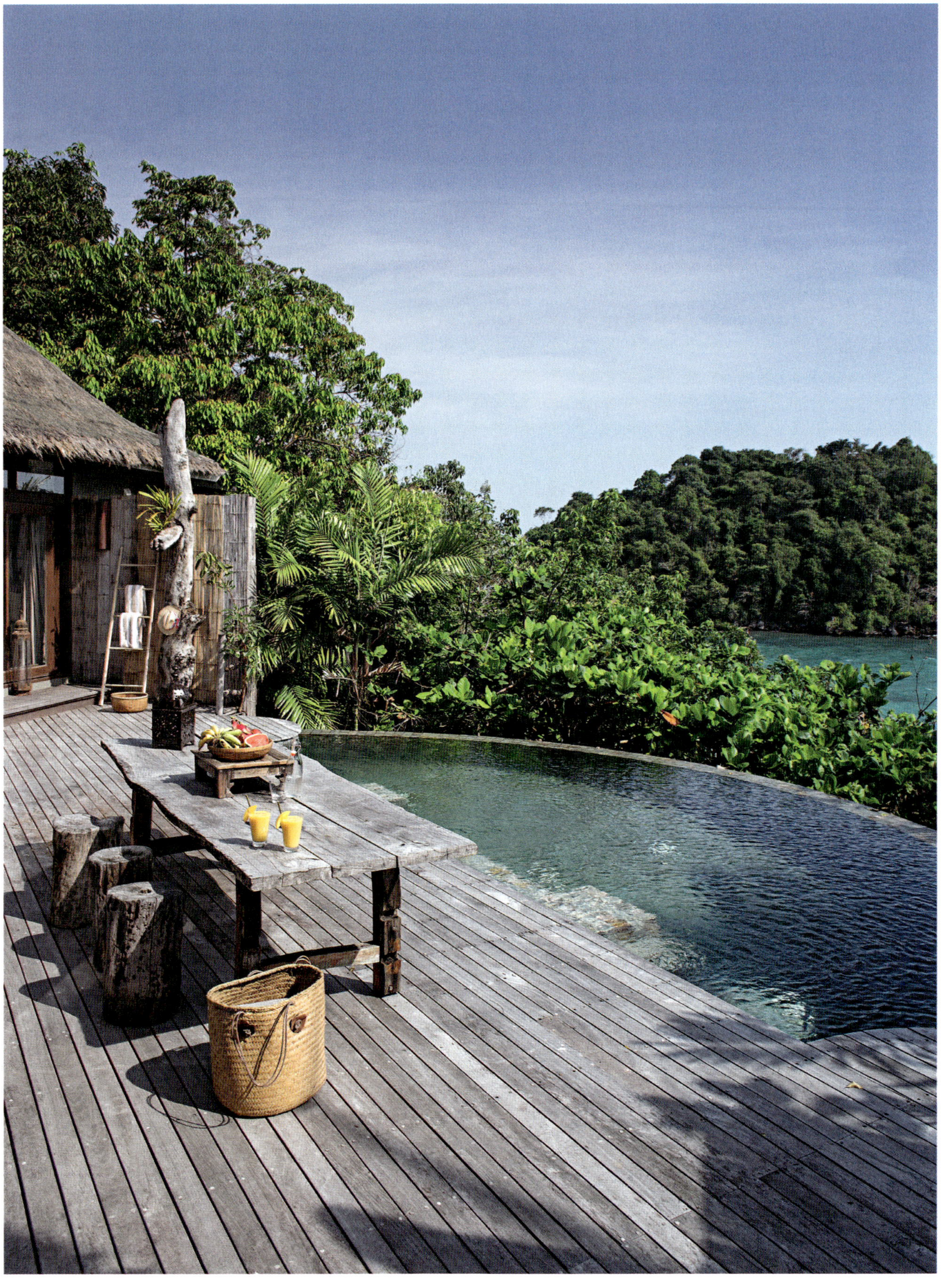

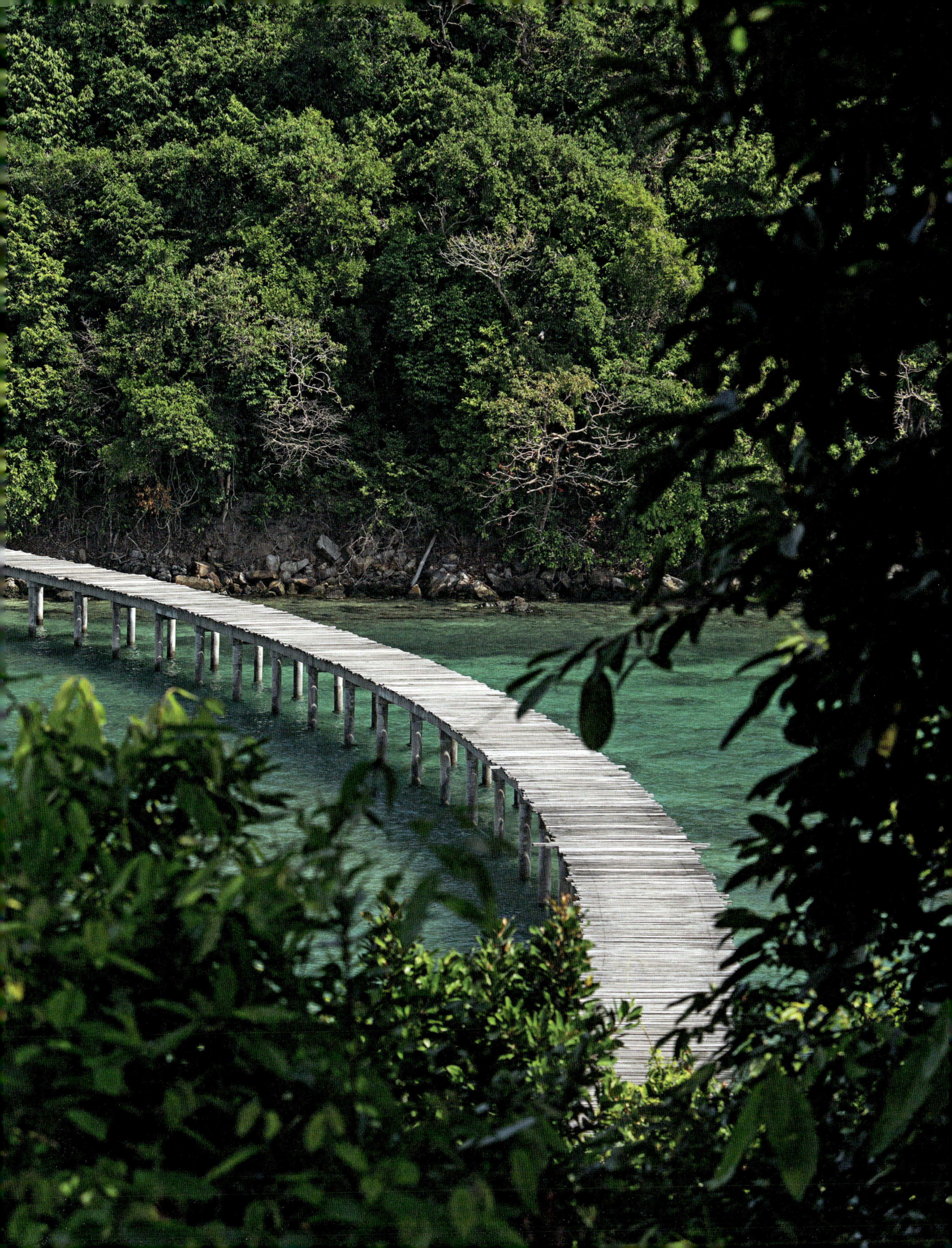

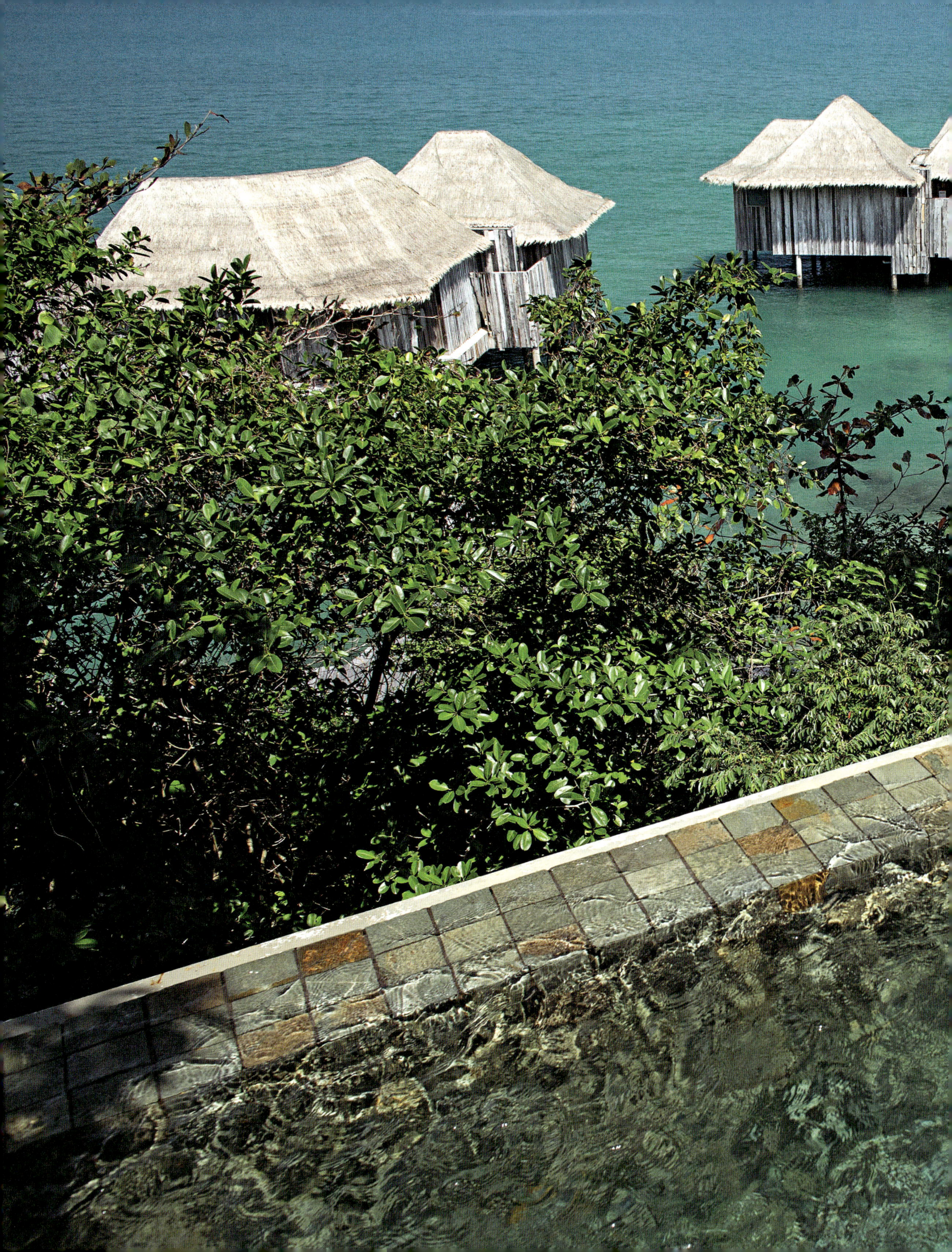

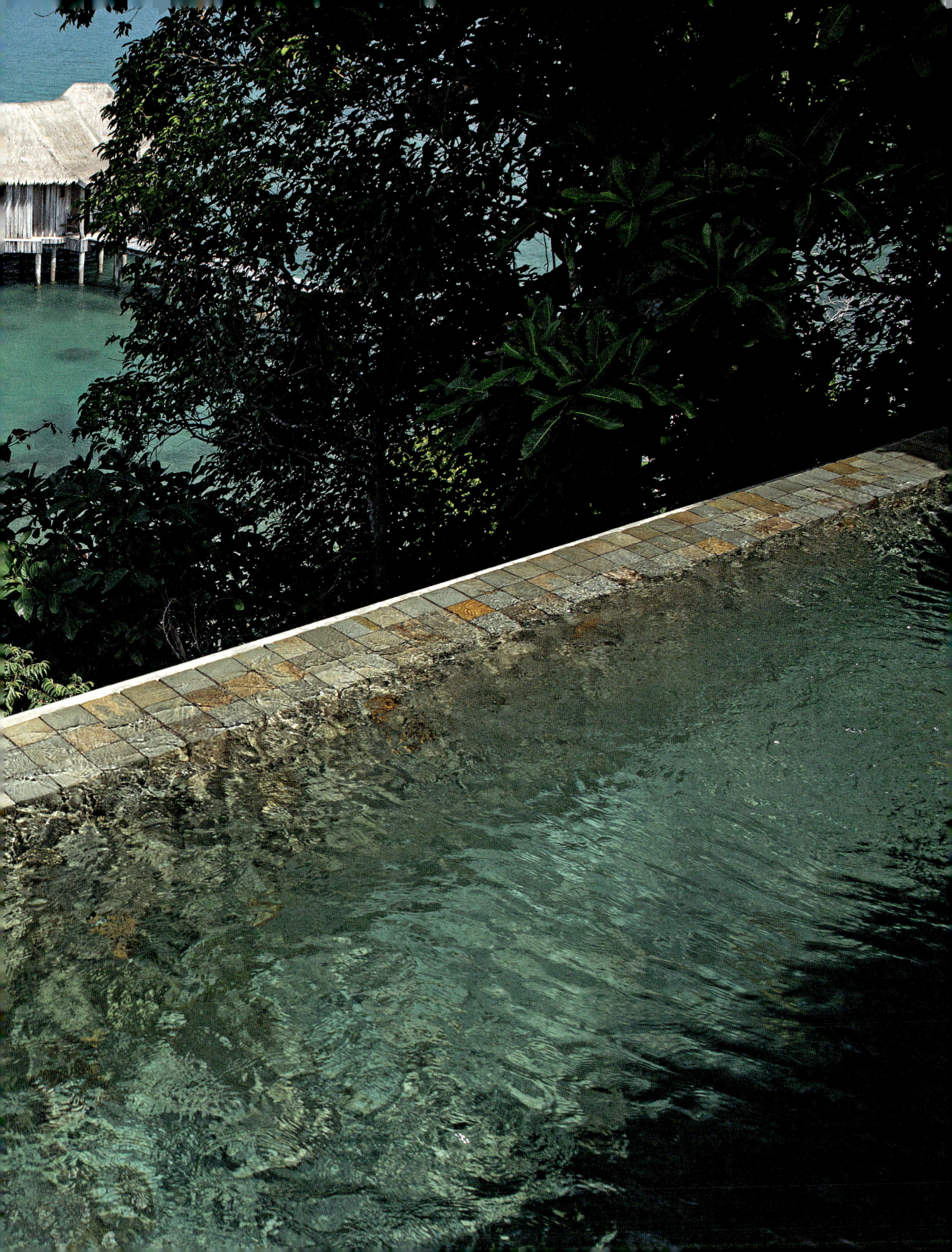

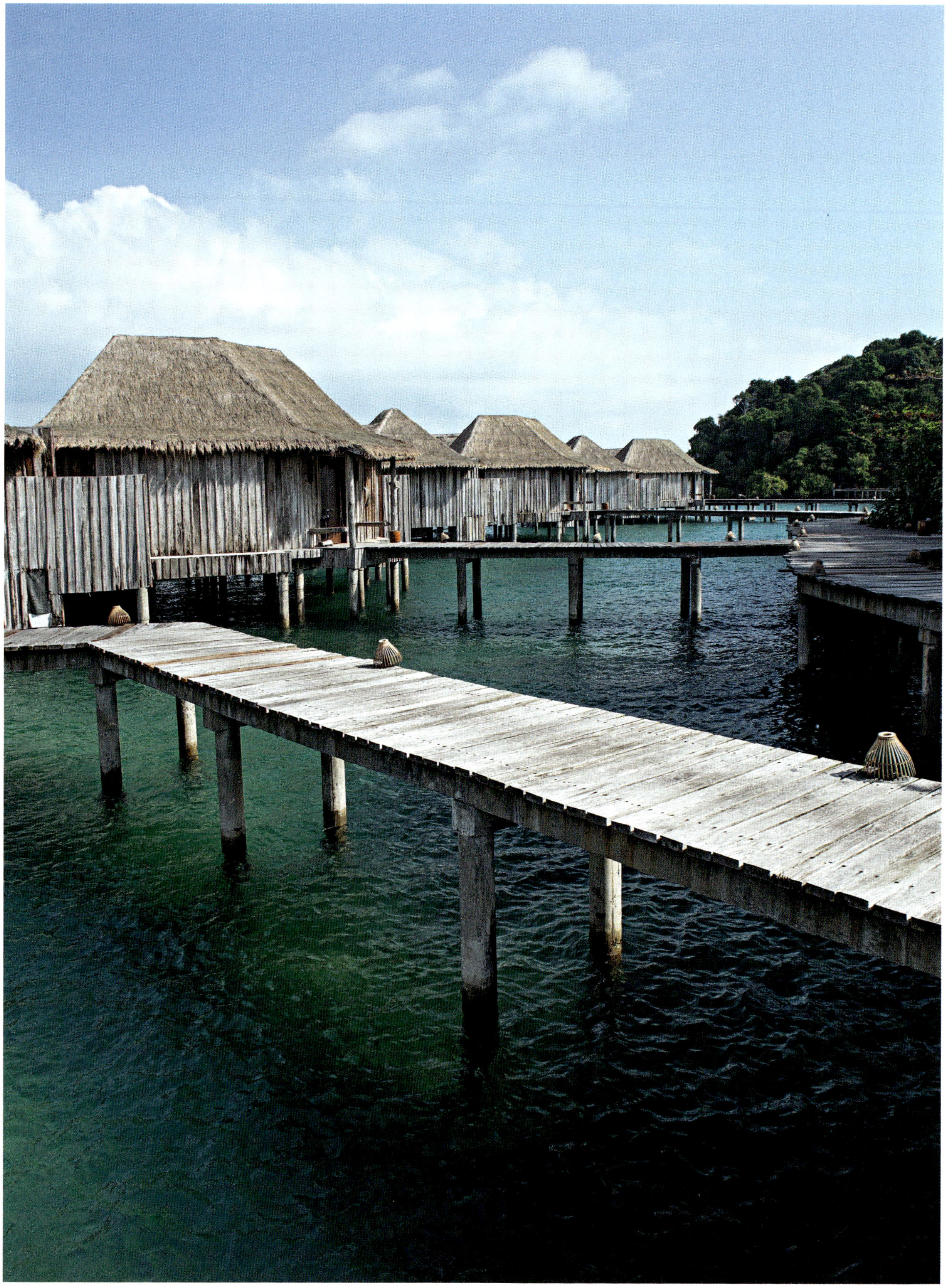

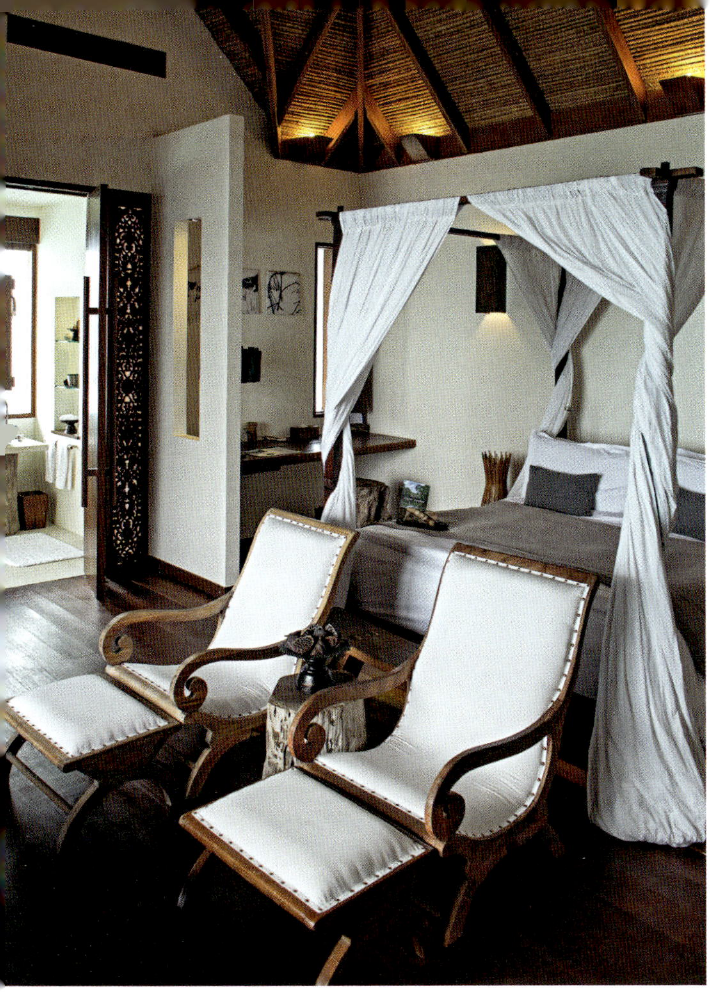
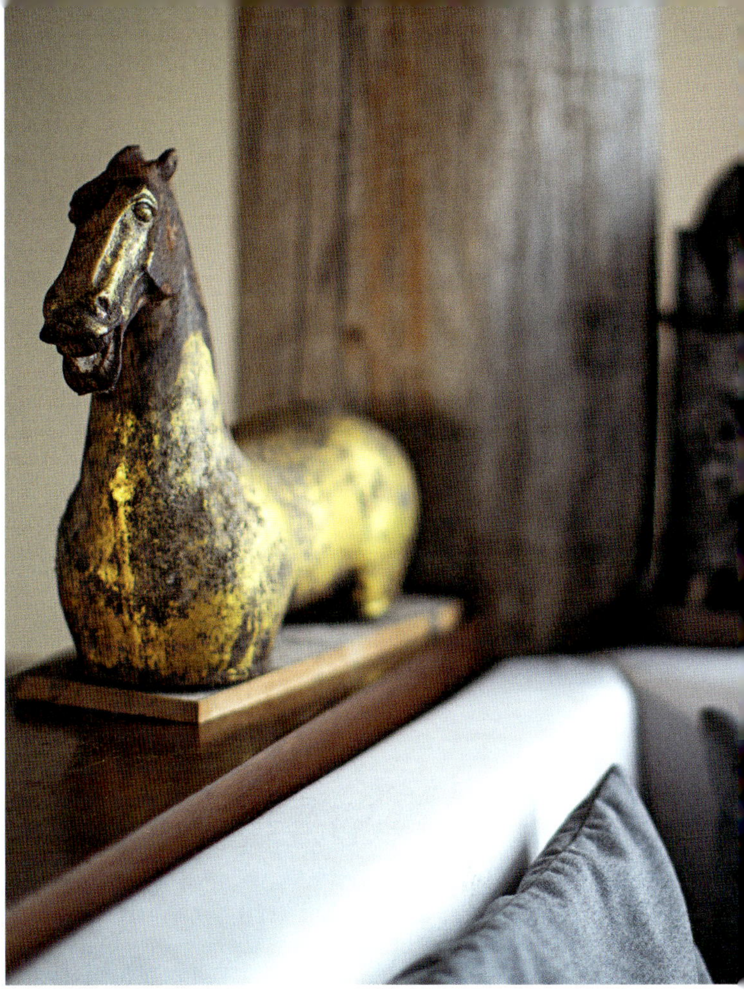
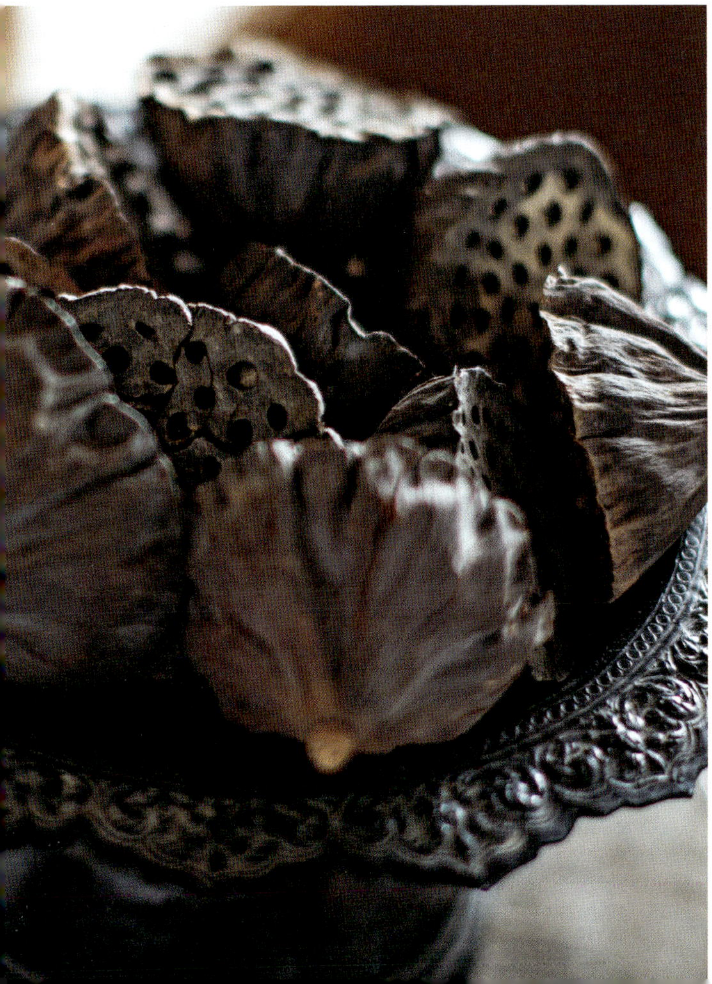
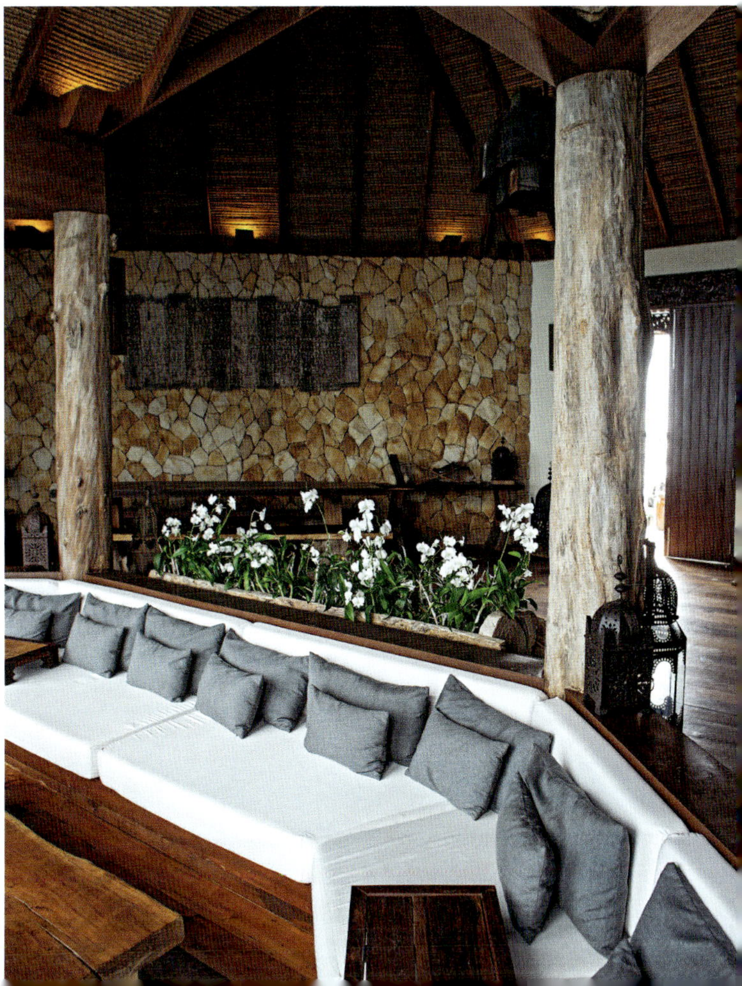

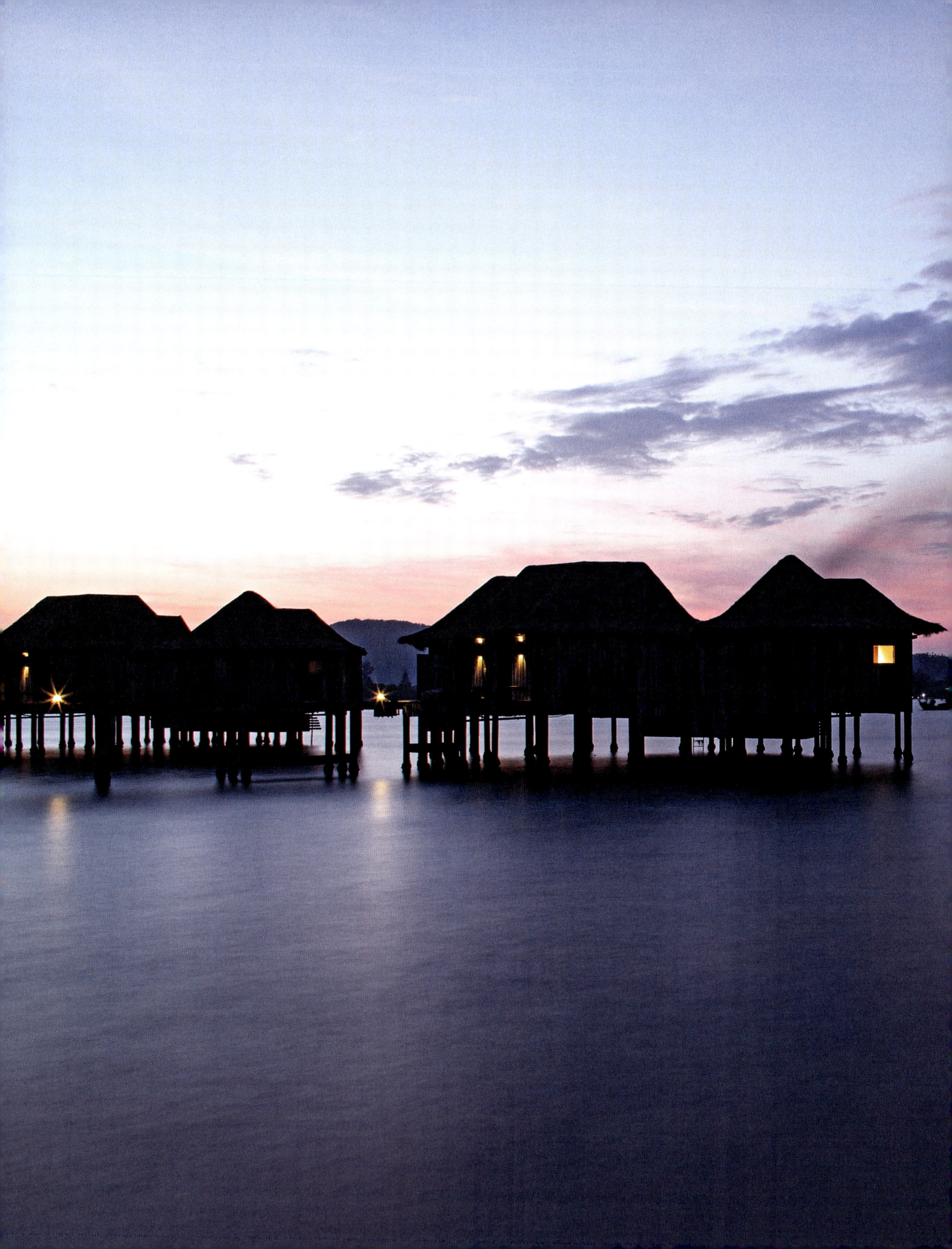

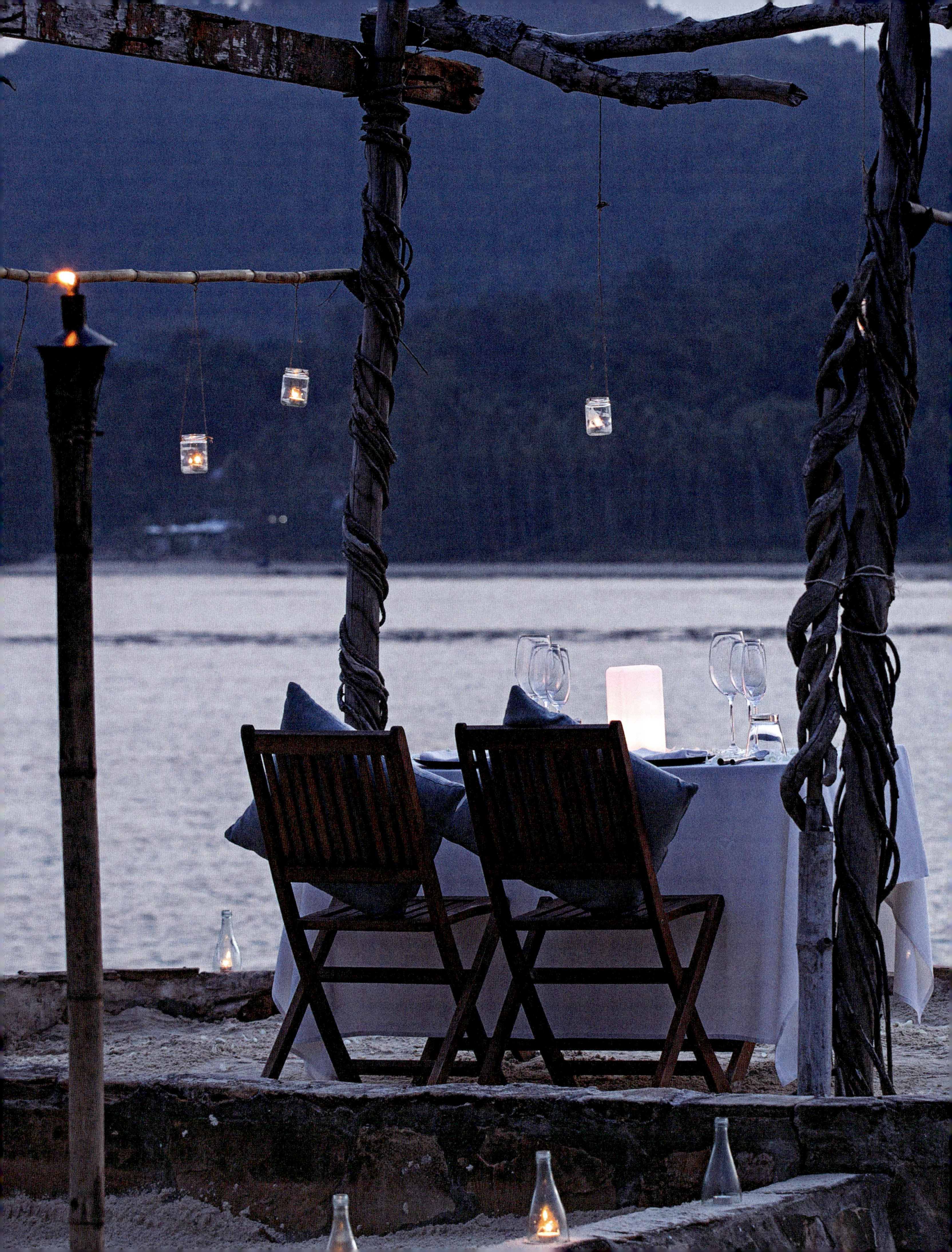

SONG SAA DINNER

FISH AMOK

INGREDIENTS / serves 4

600 g (1lb 5 oz) white fish fillet

1 tsp salt

1 tsp pepper

4 tbsp cooking oil

200 g (1 cup) amok paste

500 g (2 cups) coconut cream

2 tbsp fish sauce

1 tsp palm sugar

TO SERVE

steamed rice

TO GARNISH

6 Thai basil leaves

METHOD

Cut the fish fillets into cubes, then season with salt and pepper. Heat 2 tablespoons oil in a frying pan over a high heat, add the fish cubes and sear for 1 minute. Remove and set aside.

Heat the remaining oil in a medium-sized frying pan. Add the amok paste and cook for 1 minute over a medium heat. Add the coconut cream and bring to a boil, then reduce the heat. Add the fish sauce and the palm sugar and simmer for 1–2 minutes.

Add the fish to the frying pan and cook for 3–4 minutes.

Arrange the fish on 4 plates or in banana baskets with the steamed rice.

Garnish with basil, then serve.

SONG SAA DINNER

SONG SAA DINNER

PRAWN LAKSA

INGREDIENTS / serves 4

500 g (1 lb) raw prawns in their shells

2 eggs

Laksa paste (see page 43)

palm sugar to taste

fish sauce to taste

soy sauce to taste

TO SERVE

steamed rice

TO GARNISH

4 sprigs Thai basil

4 sprigs fresh coriander

4 lime wedges

METHOD

Clean the raw prawns and cut the shells along the back with a sharp knife.

In a saucepan, bring water to a boil, add the eggs and cook for 5 minutes until hard. Cool them under running cold water, then peel them. Cut the eggs in half lengthways.

Put the laksa paste into a deep saucepan and bring to a simmer. Add the prawns and cook for 5–6 minutes until they start to turn dark red and curl. Take off the heat and leave to rest for 2–3 minutes. Check the seasoning and add palm sugar, fish sauce or soy sauce to taste.

Arrange the prawns and the laksa on the plates, with half an egg for each portion. Garnish with the Thai basil, coriander and lime wedges and serve with white rice.

SEA BASS IN A COCONUT AND LIME REDUCTION

INGREDIENTS / serves 4

8 prawns

2 tbsp peanut oil

4 sea bass fillets (about 600 g / 1 lb 5 oz)

For the coconut lime reduction

4 stalks lemongrass

1 thumb-sized piece fresh galangal

4 lime leaves

200 ml (1 cup) fish stock

800 ml (4 cups) coconut milk

salt and pepper

For the mango and cashew nut salsa

1 mango

2 shallots

100 g (½ cup) cashew nuts

24 mint leaves

24 coriander leaves

40 ml (⅛ cup) lime juice

METHOD

Preheat the oven to 180°C (350°F).

To make the coconut lime reduction, cut the lemongrass into 5 cm (2 in) pieces and crush them using a pestle and mortar. Peel the galangal and also crush it. Do not chop the lime leaves. Put all the ingredients into a saucepan and simmer for 30 minutes until the sauce thickens. Strain out the galangal, lime leaves and lemongrass. Season with salt and pepper, then set aside.

Bring a saucepan of salted water to a boil. Add the prawns and blanch for 15 seconds or until they start curling. Set aside.

Put the oil into an ovenproof hot frying pan, add the sea bass, skin side down, and sear until the skin becomes crisp. Transfer the frying pan to the oven for 4–6 minutes until the sea bass is tender.

Meanwhile, make the mango and cashew nut salsa. Peel and dice the mango and the shallots. Toast and chop the cashew nuts. Chop the mint and coriander leaves. Combine all the ingredients for the salsa just before serving.

Serve the sea bass fillets and the prawns with a little coconut reduction and salsa on the side.

SONG SAA DINNER

SONG SAA DINNER

RED SNAPPER WITH GREEN CURRY

INGREDIENTS / serves 4

4 red snapper fillets (about 600 g / 1 lb 5 oz), with the skin

2 tbsp cooking oil

200 g (1 cup) green curry paste (see page 40)

4 sprigs fresh coriander

4 sprigs fresh mint

4 sprigs fresh Thai basil

20 ml (⅛ cup) lime juice

coconut milk (optional)

TO SERVE

steamed rice

METHOD

Preheat the oven to 180°C (350°F).

With a sharp knife, score 5 or 6 cuts into the snapper skins.

Heat the oil in an ovenproof frying pan, add the snapper fillets, skin side down, and sear. Cook until the skin is crisp, then turn over and place the frying pan in the oven for 5–8 minutes, depending on the thickness of the fillets.

Meanwhile, heat the curry paste in a saucepan and season to taste. Chop the coriander, mint and basil. Stir the lime juice and the chopped herbs into the paste. If you prefer a creamier consistency, stir a few teaspoons of water, stock or coconut milk into the paste.

Serve the fish with the green curry paste and steamed rice.

RED SNAPPER EN PAPILLOTE

INGREDIENTS / serves 4

4 red snapper fillets
(about 600 g / 1 lb 6 oz)

For the marinade

8 kaffir lime leaves

40 g (⅛ cup) chopped garlic

40 g (⅛ cup) chopped shallots

20 g (1½ tbsp) chopped galangal

2 tsp oyster sauce

4 tsp soy sauce

½ tsp salt

½ tsp pepper

1 tsp sugar

For the fish parcels

4 stalks lemongrass

4 banana leaves or sheets of baking paper

TO GARNISH

Spring onions and fresh coriander

METHOD

To make the marinade, chop the lime leaves, then combine all the marinade ingredients in a bowl. Add the fish fillets and marinate for 5 minutes.

Preheat the oven to 200°C (400°F). Halve the lemongrass lengthways. On a flat surface, lay out the banana leaves or baking paper sheets (23 x 28 cm / 9 x 11 in).

Place one fish fillet and two lemongrass halves onto the lower third of each banana leaf or sheet of paper. Fold over and crimp the edges tightly together. Place the parcels on a baking sheet and bake for 6–8 minutes, depending on the thickness of the fillets.

Take the parcels out of the oven and carefully cut open the leaves or paper. Garnish with spring onions and coriander and serve.

Tip – Instead of red snapper, you can use sea bass or any other white fish fillets, as well as whole fish or tofu in this recipe. If you are using a whole fish, such as a whole sea bass weighing 800 g–1 kg (1 lb 12 oz–2 lbs 3 oz), bake it for 30 minutes. Serve hot with rice or a salad.

SONG SAA DINNER

SONG SAA DINNER

WOK-FRIED CHICKEN WITH HOT BASIL

INGREDIENTS / serves 4

4 chicken breast fillets, skinned

salt and pepper

500 ml (2 cups) peanut oil

12 stems Thai hot basil

300 g (10 oz) long beans

4 stalks lemongrass

1 thumb-sized piece fresh galangal

6 garlic cloves

4 shallots

1 kaffir lime

2 chilies

1 long chili

2 tbsp fish sauce

2 tbsp oyster sauce

2 tbsp sweet soy sauce

½ tsp salt

1 tsp palm sugar

125 ml (½ cup) stock or water

TO SERVE

steamed rice

METHOD

Season the chicken fillets all over with salt and pepper, then cut them into cubes. Pour most of the peanut oil into a saucepan and bring to a medium heat. Add the chicken cubes and deep-fry them for about 10 minutes, then add the basil. Set aside and keep warm.

Trim the beans and cut them into thirds. Bring a saucepan of salted water to a boil, add the beans and blanch for 2–3 minutes, then drain and transfer them to a bowl with iced water to stop the cooking.

Trim the lemongrass and peel the galangal, then cut both into large chunks that can be removed from the frying pan later on. Peel and chop the garlic and the shallots. Cut 12 long, thin strips off the kaffir lime. Cut the chilies into long, thin strips. Chop the long chili.

Bring a wok to a medium high heat, add the rest of the peanut oil, lemongrass, galangal, garlic, shallots, kaffir lime strips, chilies, the long chili and the beans. Stir-fry for 1 minute, then stir in the fish sauce, oyster sauce, sweet soy sauce, salt, sugar and the stock or water.

Just before serving, remove the lemongrass and galangal chunks. Arrange the vegetables on the plates and place the fried chicken on top, garnish with the fried basil and serve with white rice.

CHICKEN IN PANDAN LEAVES

INGREDIENTS / serves 4

800 g (1 ¾ lb) chicken breast fillets

For the Khmer dressing

120 g (½ cup) pineapple

1 tsp chili

2 tbsp garlic

For the pandan marinade

2 frozen stalks lemongrass

6 frozen pandan leaves

50 g (2 cups) mint leaves

1 lime

40 g (⅛ cup) ginger

40 g (⅛ cup) garlic

4 tbsp fresh coriander leaves

4 tbsp fish sauce

1 tbsp white pepper

1 tbsp soy sauce

40 g (⅛ cup) palm sugar

2 tbsp sesame oil

TO SERVE

steamed rice

METHOD

To make the Khmer dressing, cut the pineapple into small cubes. Chop the chili and the garlic. Combine all three.

To make the marinade, cut the lemongrass and 2 pandan leaves into big chunks so you can remove them from the marinade later on. Place the remaining ingredients into a blender and mix until you have a smooth mixture. Stir the lemongrass and pandan chunks into the mixture.

Cut each chicken breast fillet into 4 equal-sized pieces and place them into the marinade for 2 hours.

Preheat the oven to 180°C / 350°F.

Place the chicken pieces and the marinade in a roasting dish and cook in the oven for around 6–7 minutes. Take the chicken out of the oven and leave to rest for 3 minutes. Remove the pandan leaves and the lemongrass.

Serve the chicken on the remaining pandan leaves, spoon over the Khmer dressing and serve with white rice.

SONG SAA DINNER

SONG SAA DINNER

BEEF LOK LAK

INGREDIENTS / serves 4

800 g (1 ¾ lbs) beef fillet

8 tbsp cooking oil

For the marinade

½ tsp salt

2 tsp palm sugar

½ tsp pepper

2 tbsp fish sauce

4 tbsp soy sauce

6 tbsp oyster sauce

2 tbsp chopped ginger

2 tbsp chopped garlic

For the black pepper sauce

2 tbsp chopped ginger

2 tbsp chopped garlic

2 tsp salt

2 tsp sugar

2 tbsp black pepper

2 tbsp fresh lime juice

TO SERVE

16 lettuce leaves

8 tomatoes, sliced

1 onion, sliced

METHOD

Cut the beef into cubes. In a large bowl, combine all the ingredients for the marinade, add the beef and marinate for a short while.

Heat the cooking oil in a frying pan over a high heat, add the beef with the marinade and fry for a few minutes until medium rare. Remove and leave to rest for 1 minute before serving.

Combine all the ingredients for the black pepper sauce.

Arrange the beef on the plates with the lettuce, tomatoes and onion and serve the black pepper sauce as an accompaniment.

PORK RIBS WITH CHILI RELISH

INGREDIENTS / serves 4

1 kg (2 lb) pork ribs

2 tbsp bird's eye chili relish

125 g (1 cup) all-purpose flour

salt and pepper

250–500 ml (2–4 cups) peanut oil

TO SERVE

125 ml (½ cup) sweet chili sauce

salad

METHOD

Chop the pork ribs into 2,5–4 cm (1–1½ in) pieces. Place the ribs in a bowl. Add the bird's eye chili relish and stir well to combine. Marinate in the fridge for at least 1 hour or up to 24 hours.

Put the flour into a second bowl and season with salt and pepper. Take the ribs out of the fridge and, with as much of the relish as possible, gently turn them in the flour until well coated all over. Place the ribs on a plate.

In a wok, heat the oil – which should be at least a thumb deep – over a high heat. When the oil begins to sizzle, carefully place the first few ribs in the oil. Do not move them for the first minute of frying. Reduce the heat to medium. Fry the ribs for 5–6 minutes on each side until they are a deep golden brown. Remove the ribs from the wok and drain them on kitchen paper. Repeat with the remaining ribs until all are fried.

Serve immediately, with sweet chili sauce for dipping and a salad on the side.

SONG SAA DINNER

SONG SAA DINNER

SWEET PORK BELLY

INGREDIENTS / serves 4

800 g (1 lb 12 oz) pork belly

500 ml (2 cups) vegetable stock

For the marinade

4 tbsp sweet soy sauce

4 tbsp sweet chili sauce

4 tbsp soy sauce

2 tbsp fish sauce

2 tbsp palm sugar

¼ tsp salt

1 tbsp pepper

For the relish

30 ml (2 tbsp) cooking oil

2 tbsp chopped long red chilies

2 tbsp crushed fresh green peppercorns

2 tbsp chopped spring onions

2 tbsp chopped long green chilies

2 tbsp white wine vinegar

salt

METHOD

Preheat the oven to 230°C (500°F).

To make the marinade, stir all the ingredients together in a large bowl. Score the skin of the pork belly with a sharp knife every centimetre (½ in), being careful not to cut through to the meat. Rub the marinade into the skin. Marinate for 5–6 minutes.

Take the meat out of the marinade, place it into a roasting dish and cook for 1 hour, or until it has a beautiful crust. Reduce the temperature to 150°C (300°F), add the vegetable stock and cook for another 3 hours, or until the meat is very tender.

To make the relish, put the cooking oil into a hot frying pan, add the long red chilies and sauté briefly. In a blender, purée the long red chilies and the cooking oil with the green peppercorns, spring onions, long green chilies, vinegar and some salt.

Serve the pork belly with the relish.

COCONUT-SMOKED RACK OF LAMB

INGREDIENTS / serves 4

4 small or 2 large sweet potatoes

2 eggs

100 g (½ cup) cornflour

salt and pepper

2–4 tbsp peanut oil

4 aubergines

6 tsp lime juice

250 ml (1 cup) yoghurt

salt and pepper

800 g (1¾ lb) rack of lamb

500 g (2 cups) dried coconut

For the coriander purée

200g (1 cup) fresh coriander

400 g (2 cups) mint leaves

1 chili

8 tbsp chopped garlic

4 tsp minced ginger

6 tsp lime juice

salt and pepper

500 ml (2 cups) plain yoghurt

METHOD

Grate the sweet potatoes onto a clean tea towel or kitchen paper and squeeze out the excess liquid. In a bowl, knead together the grated potatoes with the eggs and the cornflour. Season with salt and pepper. Shape the mixture into balls the size of a ping-pong ball. If it is too moist, add some more flour, a tablespoon at a time, until they stick together.

Pour 2 tablespoons of oil into a large frying pan and place it over a high heat. Put 4–5 potato balls into the pan, flatten them and fry for 5–6 minutes on each side until crisp, browned and cooked through. Drain on kitchen paper and keep warm while you repeat with the remaining oil and potato balls.

Pierce the skins of the aubergines with a fork, then grill over the flame of a gas hob until the skin is charred. Put them into a bowl and cover with cling film to steam for 15 minutes. Rub the aubergines under running cold water to remove the blackened skin. Mix the aubergines in a blender with the lime juice and the yoghurt. Season with salt and pepper. Keep warm.

Preheat the oven to 180°C (350°F). Wash and pat dry the lamb. Line a wok with a large sheet of aluminium foil with the edges overhanging. Spread the dried coconut over the foil, being careful not to let it touch the wok. Place a wire rack over the coconut inside the wok and put the wok into the oven. Once the coconut starts to smoke, place the lamb onto the wire rack and fold the foil over the top to cover it tightly. Smoke the lamb for 15 minutes, without opening the foil.

In a blender, mix the coriander, mint, chili, garlic, ginger and lime juice, then season with salt and pepper.

Take the foil off the lamb and continue roasting for 8–10 minutes until medium rare. Remove from the oven and set aside to rest for 5 minutes. Cut the lamb into individual cutlets.

Arrange the aubergine purée, potato pancakes and coriander purée on the plates. Place the lamb on top and season.

SAUTÉED PRAWNS WITH CHILI RELISH

INGREDIENTS / serves 4

4 garlic cloves

2 shallots

1 thumb-sized piece fresh ginger

120 ml (½ cup) peanut oil

1 kg (2 lb) prawns

2 tbsp bird's eye chili relish

salt and pepper

TO GARNISH

½ bunch fresh coriander, chopped

2 spring onions, chopped

METHOD

Peel and chop the garlic, shallots and ginger.

Heat the oil in a wok over a medium heat. Add the garlic, shallots and ginger and cook for 1–2 minutes until soft but not browned.

Add the prawns and cook for about 2 minutes, stirring frequently, until they are bright pink. Increase the heat to medium, and add the bird's eye chili relish and 120 ml (½ cup) water. Continue cooking until most of the water has evaporated, then remove from the heat.

Season the prawns with salt and pepper, if necessary. Garnish with the coriander and the spring onions and serve.

Tip – The prawns taste great with rice or a salad.

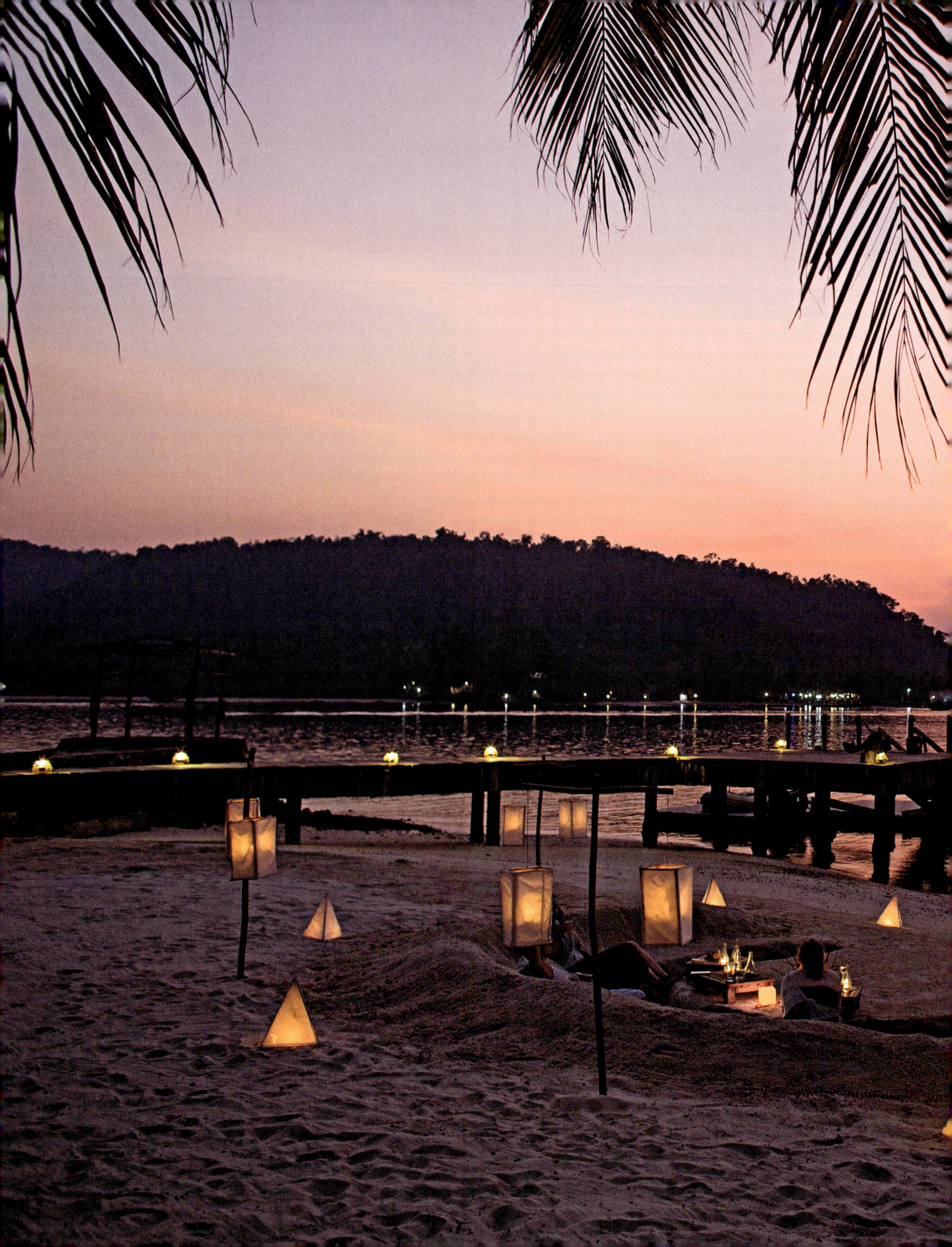

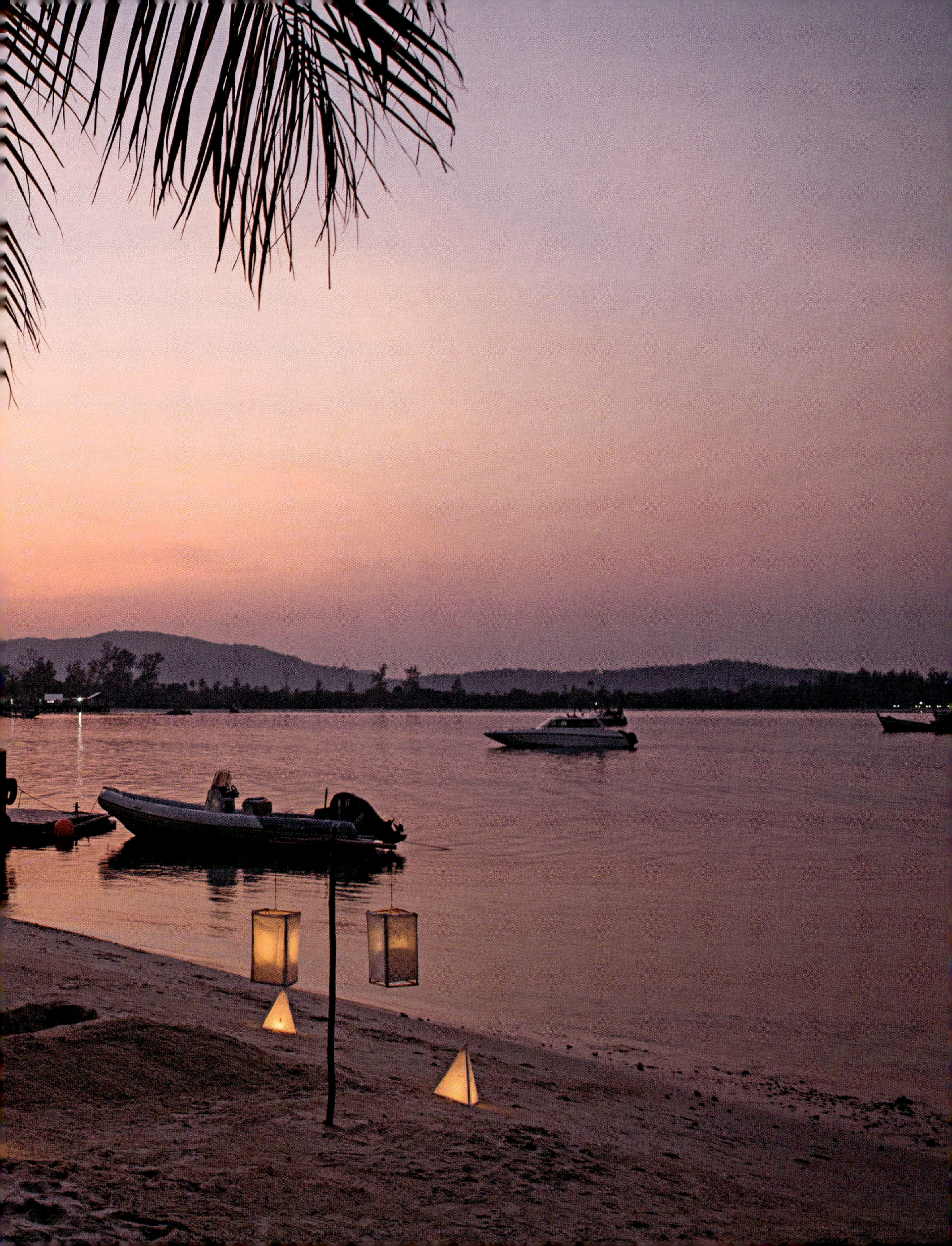

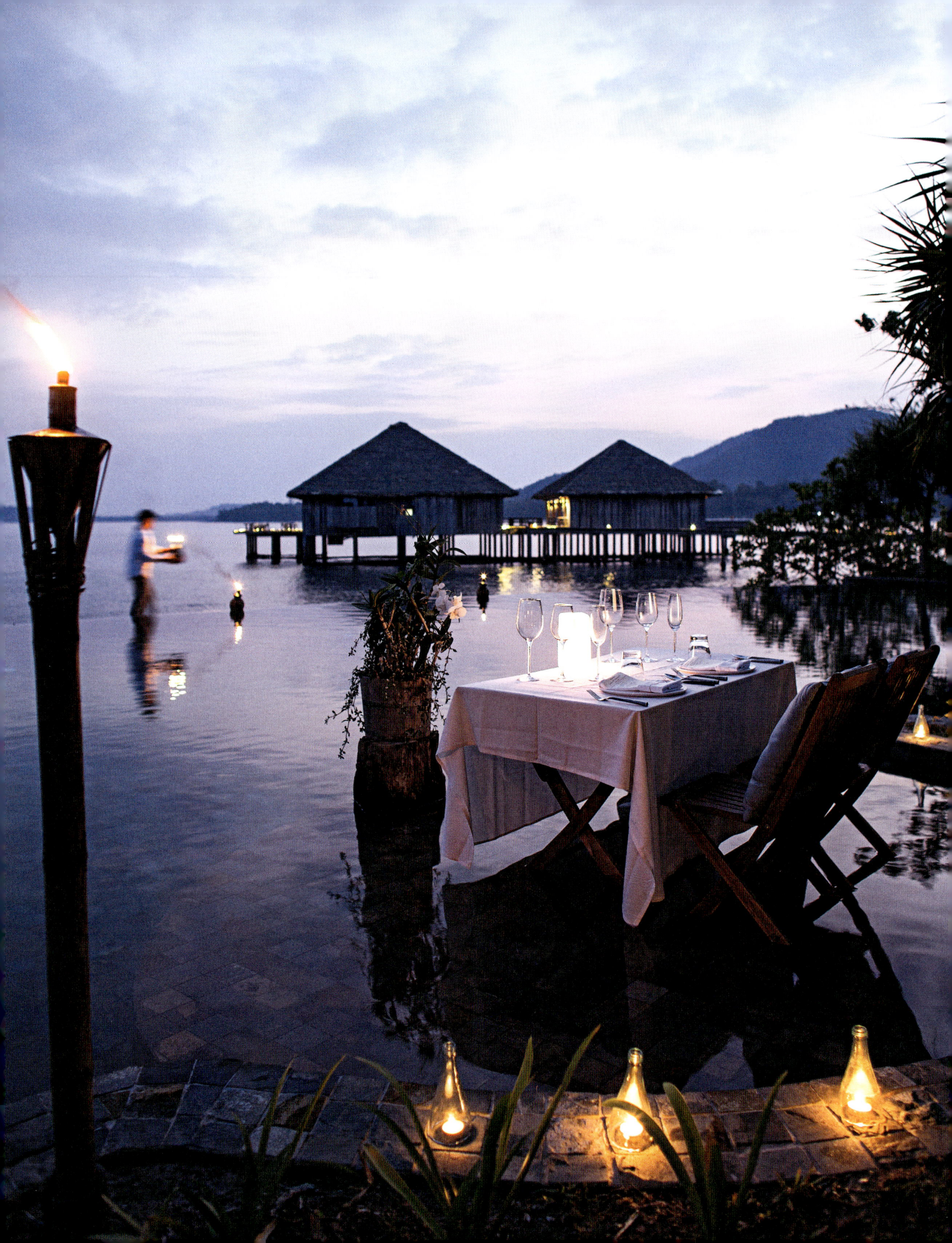

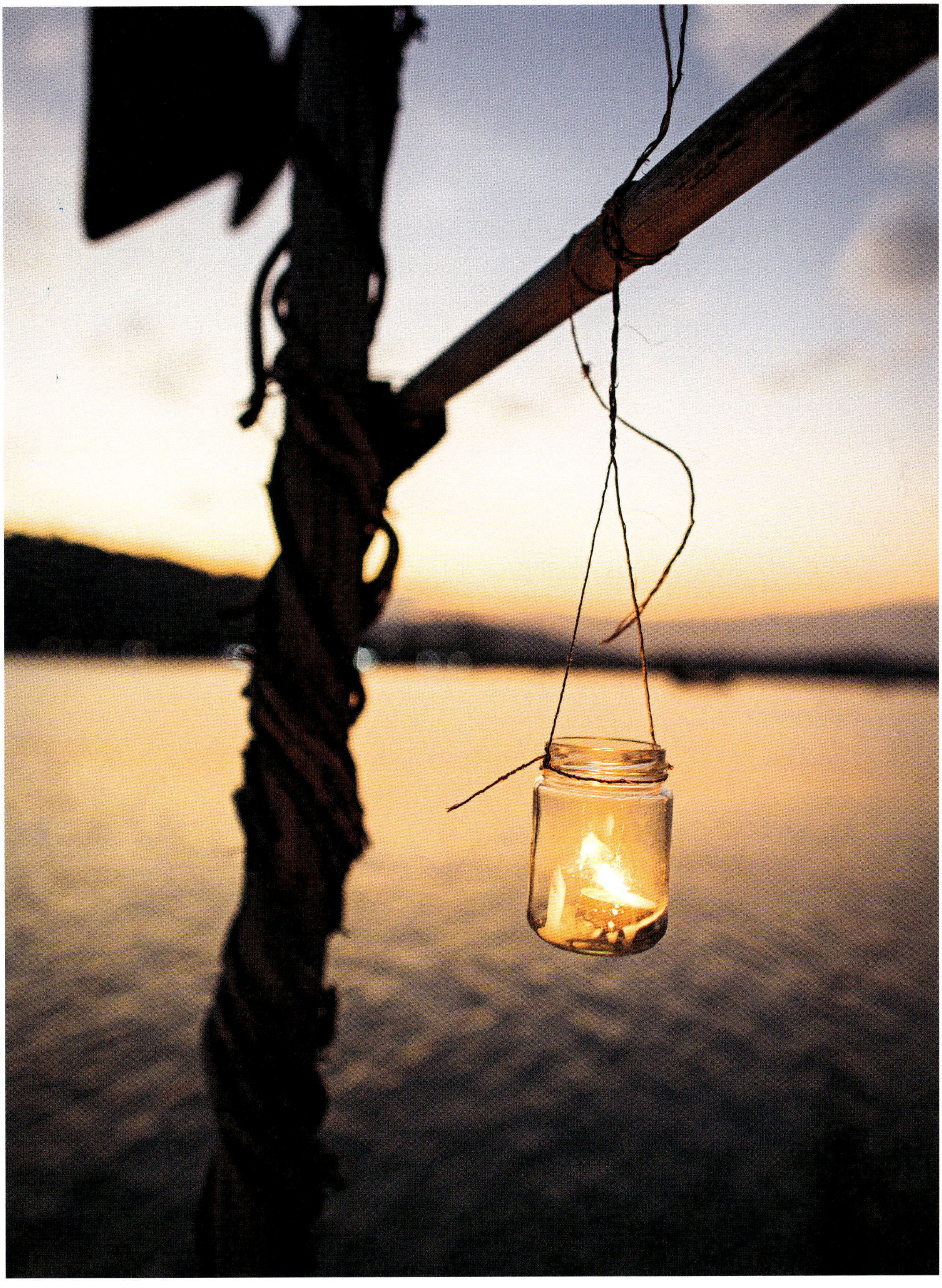

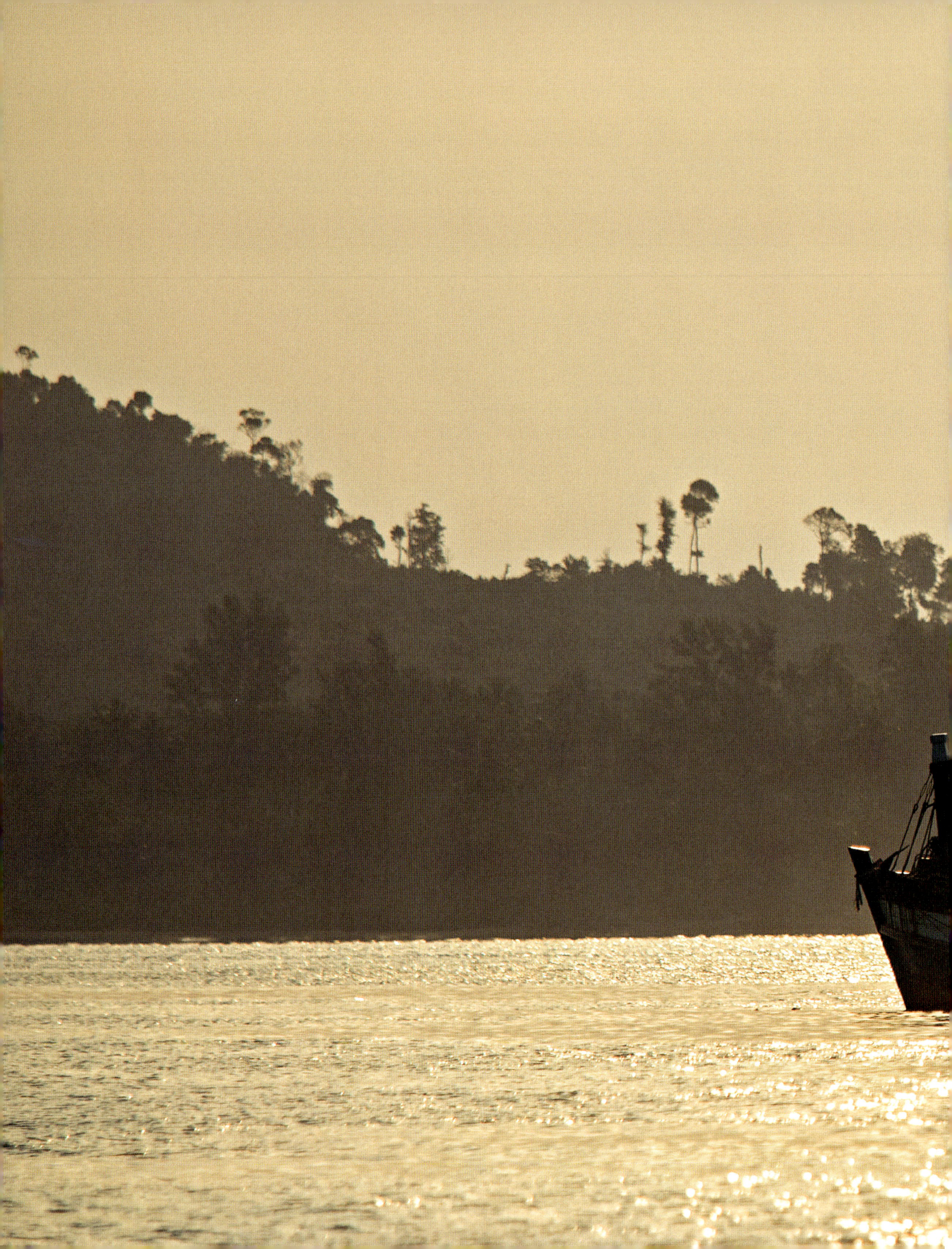

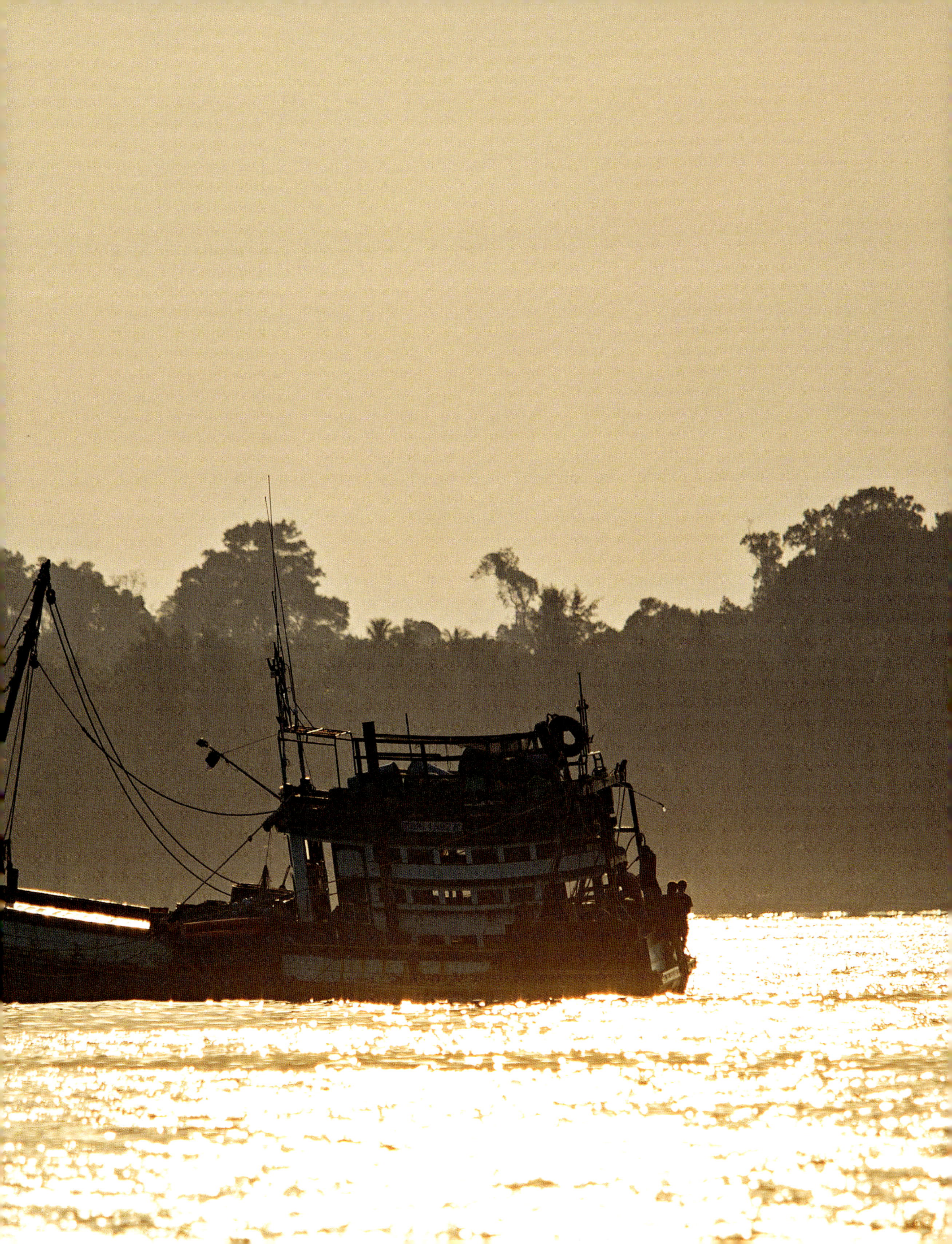

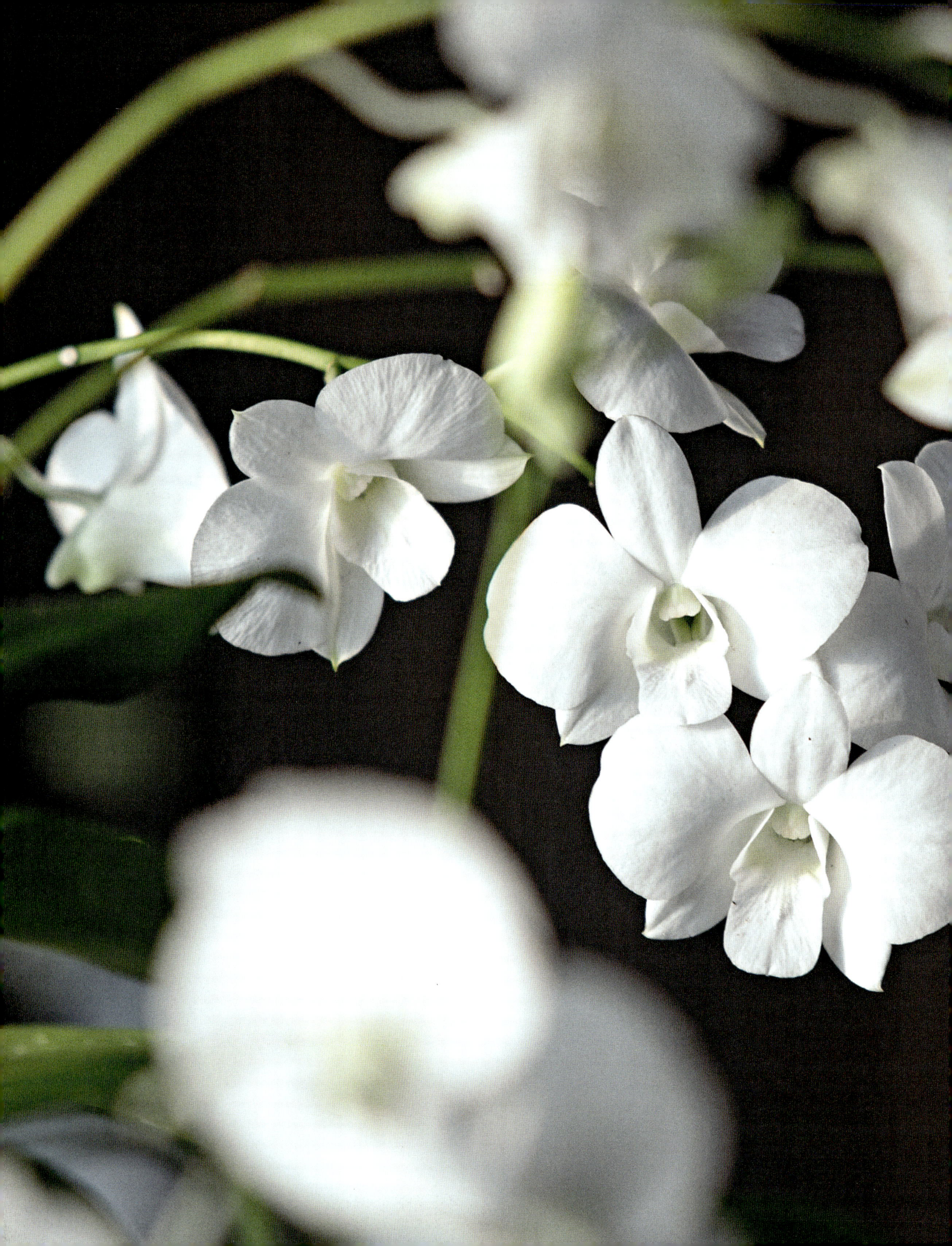

SONG SAA SWEETS

ROASTED PINEAPPLE

INGREDIENTS / serves 8

1 l (4¼ cups) pineapple juice

1 lime leaf

7 sheets gelatine

1 pineapple

60 g (4 tbsp) grated coconut

60 g (4 tbsp) cashew nuts

METHOD

Put the pineapple juice and the lime leaf into a saucepan and heat. Follow the instructions on the gelatine packet to make 1 litre (4¼ cups) gelatine. Add the gelatine to the pineapple juice and lime leaf. Do not allow to boil, just warm. Strain through a sieve into a rectangular dish. The gelatine should not come up higher than 2 cm (¾ in) in the dish. Leave to cool overnight.

Preheat the oven to 180°C (350°F). Peel and clean the pineapple, then cut it into 2 cm (¾ in) thick slices and remove the core. Place the slices on a baking tray lined with baking paper and roast in the oven for 20 minutes. Remove and chill in the fridge.

Spread the grated coconut and the cashew nuts separately in single layers onto a baking tray and toast in the preheated oven for about 8–12 minutes. Finely chop the nuts and combine with the coconut.

Just before serving, cut the jelly into 2 cm (¾ in) cubes. Place a slice of pineapple on each plate, put the jelly cubes on top and sprinkle each portion with a tablespoon of the coconut and cashew nut mixture, then serve.

SONG SAA SWEETS

SONG SAA SWEETS

SWEET POTATO PUDDING WITH TAPIOCA

INGREDIENTS / serves 4

120 g (½ cup) small pearl tapioca

500 g (1 lb) sweet potatoes

50 g (¼ cup) coconut cream

350 g (1½ cup) coconut milk

3–4 tbsp palm sugar

½ tsp salt

4 tbsp coconut flakes, to serve (optional)

METHOD

Bring a medium-sized saucepan of water to a boil and add the tapioca. Boil for 2–3 minutes, then cover and reduce the heat to medium-low. Cook covered for 15 minutes, stirring occasionally to prevent sticking. After 15 minutes take the saucepan off the heat but leave the tapioca in the water while preparing the rest.

Peel the sweet potatoes and cut them into 1 cm (⅓ in) cubes. Once peeled, sweet potatoes quickly discolour so make sure you have everything ready or soak them in cold water while you continue.

In a large saucepan, bring 500 ml (2 cups) water to a boil, then add the sweet potato cubes. Reduce the heat and simmer for about 15 minutes, or until the sweet potatoes are tender. Drain the cubes, reserving the cooking water.

Add the coconut cream, coconut milk and sugar to the water and bring back to a boil, stirring well. Simmer for 5–7 minutes, then take off the stove and leave to cool.

Drain the tapioca and rinse under cold water, then drain again and add to the coconut mixture together with the sweet potato cubes. Stir to combine and season with the salt.

Top with some coconut flakes, if you like, and serve.

TARO AND STICKY RICE PUDDING

INGREDIENTS / serves 4

120 g (½ cup) sticky rice, uncooked

500 g (1 lb) taro

50 g (¼ cup) coconut cream

350 g (1½ cup) coconut milk

3 tbsp sugar

2 pandan leaves

½ tsp salt

4 tbsp coconut flakes

METHOD

Soak the sticky rice in water overnight. The next day, steam the sticky rice for 30 minutes, then let it cool for 10 minutes.

The next day peel the taro and cut it into 1 cm (½ in) cubes. Rinse the cubes, then put them into a saucepan with 500 ml (2 cups) water. Bring to a boil and simmer for 15 minutes, or until the taro is tender. Remove the taro cubes from the water and rinse them again. Set aside.

Add the coconut cream, coconut milk, sugar and pandan leaves to the water in the saucepan and bring to a boil. Stir well and simmer for 5–7 minutes, then remove the pandan leaves and let the mixture cool a little.

Add the taro cubes, sticky rice and salt to the coconut mixture and stir to combine well.

Let everything cool completely and leave to rest for at least 20 minutes. The rice will continue to absorb the liquid and become ever creamier and less watery in consistence.

Arrange on four plates, top each one with 1 tablespoon of coconut flakes and serve.

Tip – You can prepare this dessert in advance.

SONG SAA SWEETS

SONG SAA SWEETS

SWEET TREATS

COCONUT CHOCOLATE

INGREDIENTS
25 sweets

200 g (7 oz) desiccated coconut

200 g (7 oz) chocolate couverture

200 g (7 oz) quality dark chocolate

200 g (7 oz) leftover chocolate brownie sponge or shortbread

METHOD

Melt the dark chocolate in the microwave or in a heat-resistant saucepan over a pan of boiling water.

Crumb the chocolate brownie sponge or shortbread in a blender. Add the melted chocolate and the coconut and mix to combine.

Form small truffles with your hands, place on a tray and chill for at least 1 hour.

Melt the chocolate couverture and use to coat the truffles. Chill again.

WHITE CHOCOLATE

INGREDIENTS
25 sweets

325 g (11 oz) white chocolate

60 g (½ cup) whipping cream

25 g (¼ cup) Irish cream (e.g. Baileys)

100 g (½ cup) cashew nuts

METHOD

Preheat the oven to 180°C (350°F).

Melt the white chocolate in the microwave or in a heat-resistant bowl set over a pan of boiling water.

In a separate saucepan, bring the whipping cream to a boil, whisk together with the melted white chocolate for 2–3 minutes, then stir in the Irish cream. Put the mixture into the freezer for 30 minutes.

In the meantime, toast the nuts. Spread the cashew nuts in a single layer on a baking oven tray and toast in the oven for about 8–12 minutes. Remove them from the oven and finely chop them.

After 30 minutes, take the chocolate mixture out of the freezer. Scoop out teaspoon-sized truffles and shape them into little balls with your hands. Turn the truffles in the roasted cashew nuts to coat.

STICKY RICE

INGREDIENTS
25 sweets

300 g (5 cups) sticky rice

50 g (¼ cup) palm sugar

50 g (⅓ cup) white sugar

½ tsp salt

4 tbsp coconut milk

75 g (⅔ cup) grated coconut

METHOD

Soak the sticky rice in water overnight.

The next day, steam the sticky rice for 30 minutes, then let it cool for 10 minutes.

Put the palm sugar, white sugar, salt and coconut milk into a saucepan. Cook the mixture on a medium-high heat for 5 minutes, stirring until the sugar has completely dissolved.

Combine the sticky rice with the coconut mixture and the grated coconut and spread it on a baking tray. It should be around 1½ cm (½–¾ in) thick. Chill in the fridge for 1 hour.

Cut into little squares.

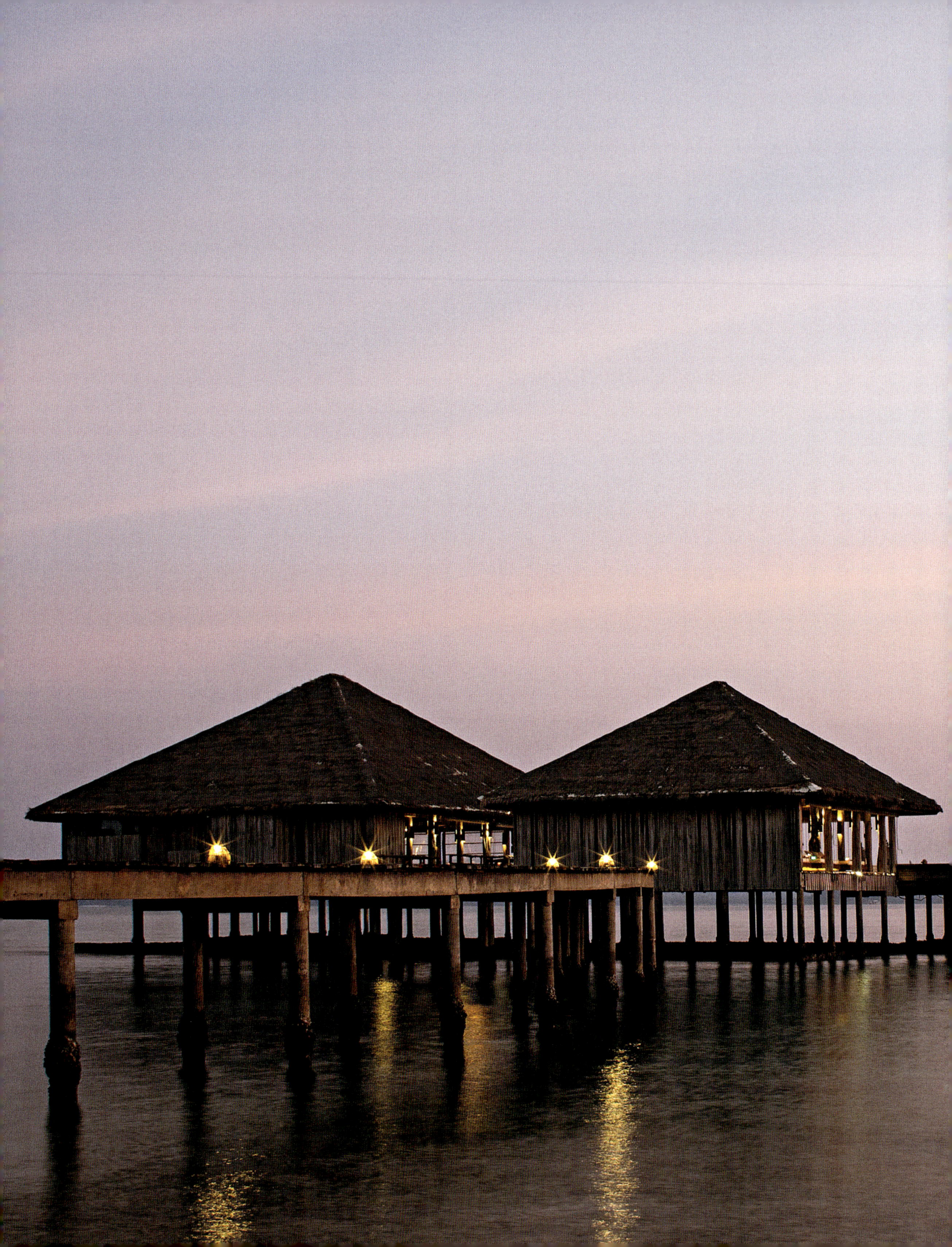

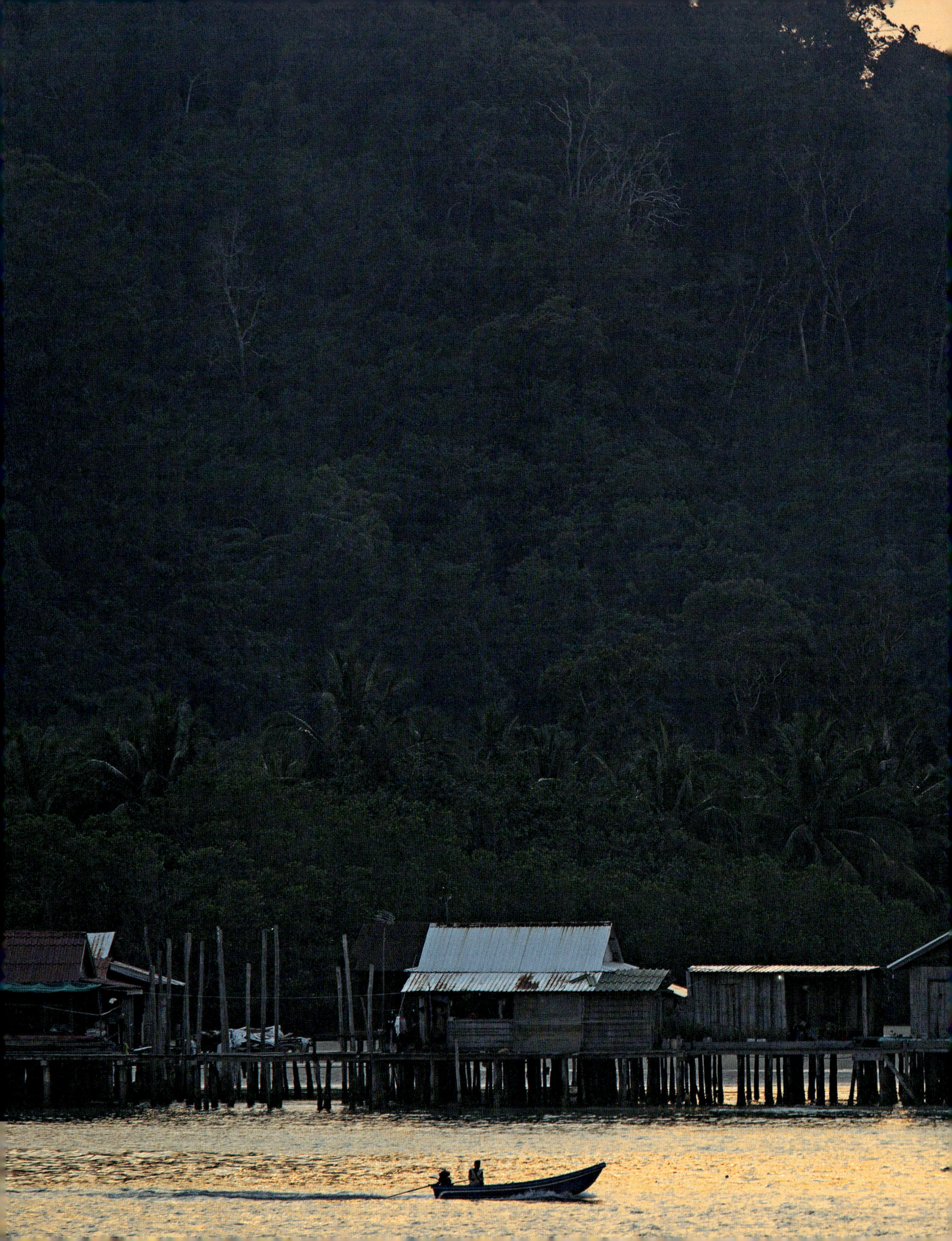

SONG SAA DRINKS

SONG SAA SUNSET

INGREDIENTS

50 ml (3 tbsp + 1 tsp) vodka

20 ml (1 tbsp + 1 tsp) lime juice

60 ml (4 tbsp) pineapple juice

10 ml (2 tsp) grenadine syrup

4 mint leaves

TO GARNISH

1 slice of pineapple, dried

METHOD

Pour all the ingredients into a cocktail shaker and shake well. Strain into a rocks glass.

Garnish with pineapple, then serve with a straw.

CLASSIC SONG SAA

INGREDIENTS

1 brown sugar cube

3 dashes Angostura

1 tsp Grand Marnier

150 ml (⅔ cup) Prosecco

TO GARNISH

1 orange twist

METHOD

Soak the sugar cube in the Angostura, then place it in a flute glass. Cover with the Grand Marnier and gently pour the Prosecco on top.

Garnish with the orange twist and serve.

SONG SAA DRINKS

SONG SAA SUNSET

SONG SAA DRINKS

PIMM'S RANGOON

PIMM'S RANGOON

INGREDIENTS

1 thumb-sized piece fresh ginger

4 cucumber sticks, thinly sliced

1 lime wedge

40 ml (2 tbsp + 2 tsp) Pimm's No.1

130 ml (8 tbsp + 2 tsp) ginger ale

TO GARNISH

1 stalk lemongrass as a swizzle stick

METHOD

Peel and roughly chop the ginger. Thinly slice the cucumber, leaving the skin on. Thinly slice the lime wedge.

In a highball glass, pile the ginger, cucumber and lime onto crushed ice cubes. Add the Pimm's and top with the ginger ale.

Add the lemongrass as a swizzle stick along with a straw, then serve.

BASIL BEAUTY

INGREDIENTS

salt and pepper

45 ml (3 tbsp) Samai Kampot Pepper Rum

75 ml (5 tbsp) grapefruit juice

20 ml (4 tbsp) pepper and basil syrup

20 ml (4 tbsp) lime juice

TO GARNISH

1 sprig basil

METHOD

On a plate, combine salt and pepper. Moisten the rim of a rocks glass and twist it in the mix. Put all the ingredients into a cocktail shaker and shake well. Pour the cocktail into the rocks glass, garnish with a fresh basil sprig and serve.

LEMONGRASS COLLINS

INGREDIENTS

1 stalk lemongrass

50 ml (4 tbsp) vodka

30 ml (2 tbsp) lime juice

1 tsp brown sugar

100 ml (½ cup) ginger ale

TO GARNISH

1 lime wedge

METHOD

Roughly shred the lemongrass.

In a cocktail shaker, combine the lemongrass, vodka, lime juice and brown sugar. Shake, then strain into a highball glass. Fill with ginger ale.

Garnish with a lime wedge and serve with a straw.

PASSIONATE DISTILLERS

INGREDIENTS

50 ml (3 tbsp + 1 tsp) Samai Gold Rum

50 ml (3 tbsp + 1 tsp) passion fruit juice

10 ml (2 tsp) vanilla syrup

soda water

TO GARNISH

1 slice passion fruit

1 sprig mint

METHOD

Fill a rocks glass with ice cubes, add the rum, passion fruit juice and vanilla syrup, then top up with soda water. Stir with a bar spoon to combine. Garnish with a fresh passion fruit slice and a mint sprig, then serve.

SONG SAA DRINKS

LEMONGRASS COLLINS

SONG SAA DRINKS

CUCUMBER PUNCH

CUCUMBER PUNCH

INGREDIENTS

½ cucumber

20 ml (4 tbsp) lime juice

crushed ice

soda water

TO GARNISH

cucumber wheel

METHOD

Peel the cucumber and blitz in a blender, then strain off the juice. Add the cucumber juice and lime juice to a shaker. Shake well, then strain over crushed ice in a rock or highball glass. Top up with soda water.

Garnish with a cucumber wheel and serve.

ISLAND COOLER

INGREDIENTS

20 ml (4 tbsp) freshly squeezed lime juice

80 g (3 oz) cucumber

30 g (1 oz) ginger, peeled

5 mint leaves

250 ml (1 cup) soda water

1 ½ honey

TO GARNISH

1 mint leaf

METHOD

Put the juice, cucumber, ginger, mint leaves, sparkling water and honey into a mixer and blend. Strain the contents into a rocks glass, garnish with a mint leaf and serve.

WATERMELON BREEZE

INGREDIENTS

90 ml (⅓ cup + 1 tbsp) fresh watermelon juice or water with watermelon syrup

70 ml (⅓ cup) pineapple juice

10 ml (2 tsp) lime juice

crushed ice

TO GARNISH

1 pandan leaf

1 watermelon wedge

straw

METHOD

In a shaker, combine all the ingredients. Shake well with the ice and strain into a highball glass.

Garnish with the pandan leaf and the watermelon wedge. Serve with a straw.

GINGER TONIC

INGREDIENTS

½ apple

30 g (1 oz) ginger

1 ½ tbsp honey

20 ml (4 tsp) lime juice

250 ml (1 cup) soda water

crushed ice

TO GARNISH

1 slice apple

METHOD

Peel the apple and the ginger and blitz in a blender, then strain off the juice. Pour the apple and ginger juice, the honey and the lime juice into a shaker. Shake well, then strain into a rocks or highball glass over crushed ice. Top up with sparkling water, garnish with an apple slice and serve.

SONG SAA DRINKS

WATERMELON BREEZE

SONG SAA DRINKS

GINGER LEMONGRASS

GINGER LEMONGRASS

INGREDIENTS

½ stalk lemongrass

1 lime wedge

2 thumb-sized pieces fresh ginger, roughly chopped

4 basil leaves

crushed ice

180 ml (¾ cup) ginger ale

TO GARNISH

basil leaves

1 stalk lemongrass as a swizzle stick

METHOD

Chop the lemongrass and the lime wedge. Peel and chop the ginger. In a shaker, combine the lemongrass, lime, ginger and basil leaves. Shake and stir, then squeeze with spoon so that the flavours fully develop.

Strain into a highball glass, add the ice and top with the ginger ale.

Garnish with basil leaves and serve with a straw and a lemongrass stalk as swizzle stick.

MANGO COOLER

INGREDIENTS

90 ml (6 tbsp) mango juice

90 ml (6 tbsp) orange juice

4 chopped mint leaves

crushed ice

TO GARNISH

1 sprig mint

METHOD

In a shaker, combine all the ingredients and shake well with the ice. Strain into a highball glass, garnish with a sprig of mint and serve with a straw.

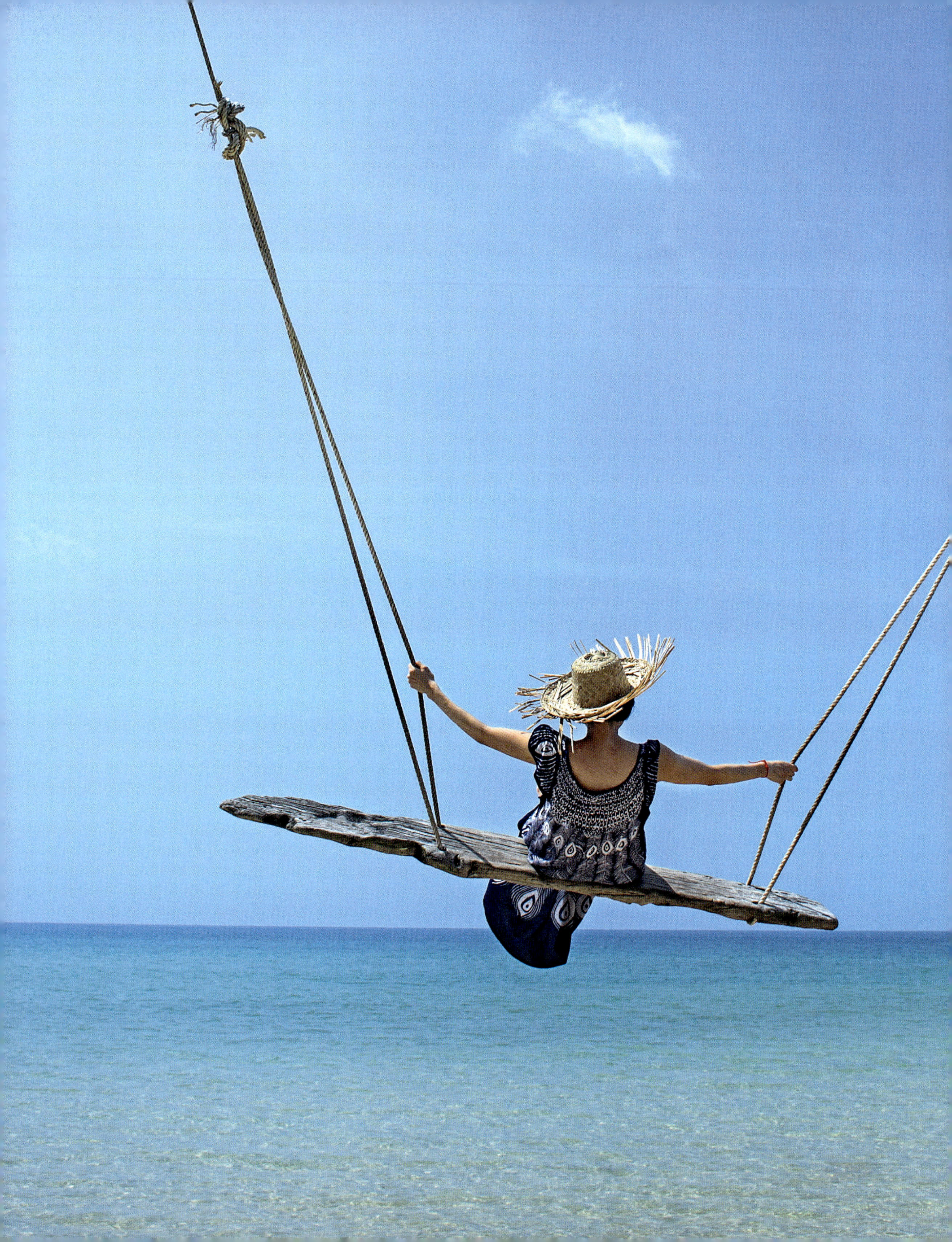

LONELY BEACH – AN EXCURSION DESTINATION

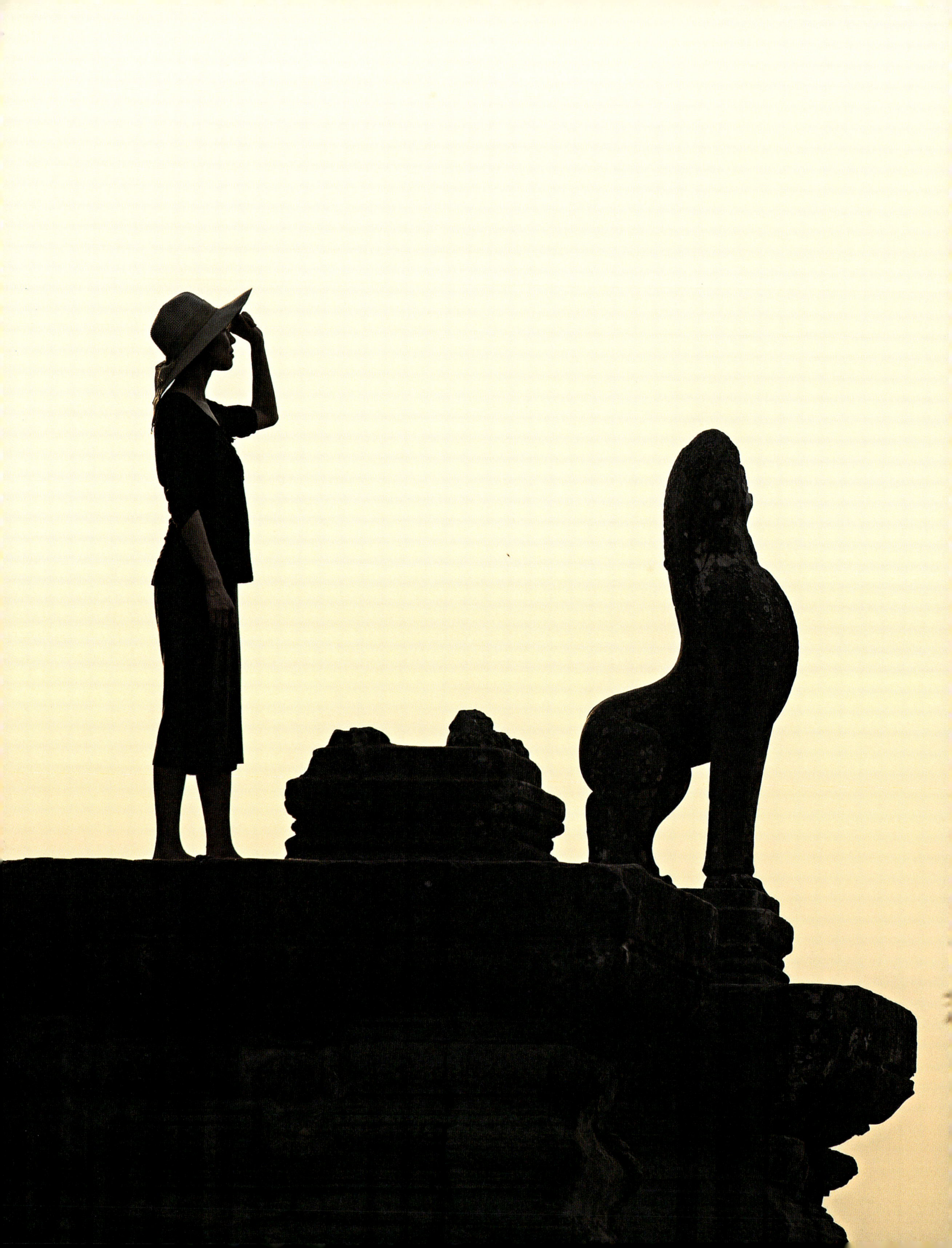

INDEX

A

AUBERGINE
Pad Thai 82
Coconut-Smoked Rack of Lamb 136

B

BEANSPROUT
Breakfast Soup Guy Teaw 54
Pad Thai 82

BEEF
Breakfast Soup Guy Teaw 54
Rice Porridge Bor Bor 58
Beef Lok Lak 130

BLACK MUSHROOM
Rice Porridge Bor Bor 58
Hot and Sour Seafood Soup 60

C

CABBAGE
Crispy Vermicelli 80

CARROT
Breakfast Soup Guy Teaw 54
Khmer Rice Cakes 66
Cambodian Mango Salad 72
Crispy Vermicelli 80

CHICKEN
Rice Porridge Bor Bor 58
Crispy Vermicelli 80
Wok-Fried Chicken with Hot Basil 126
Chicken in Pandan Leaves 128

CHOCOLATE
Coconut Chocolate 152
White Chocolate 152

COCONUT (dried, cream, milk)
Lemongrass Oatmeal 56
Khmer Rice Cakes 66
Scallop Ceviche 76
Pad Thai 82
Fish Amok 116
Sea Bass in a Coconut and Lime Reduction 120
Coconut-Smoked Rack of Lamb 136
Roasted Pineapple 146
Sweet Potato Pudding with Tapioca 148
Taro and Sticky Rice Pudding 150
Coconut Chocolate 152
Sticky Rice 152

COURGETTE
Courgette and Cucumber Salad 70

CUCUMBER
Courgette and Cucumber Salad 70
Crispy Vermicelli 80
Duck Salad with Black Sesame 84

D

DUCK
Duck Salad with Black Sesame 84

F

FISH
Breakfast Soup Guy Teaw 54
Rice Porridge Bor Bor 58
Fish Amok 116
Sea Bass in a Coconut and Lime Reduction 120
Red Snapper with Green Curry 122
Red Snapper en Papillote 124

L

LAMB
Lamb Cutles with Fresh Spinach 86
Coconut-Smoked Rack of Lamb 136

LEMONGRASS
Breakfast Soup Guy Teaw 54
Lemongrass Oatmeal 56
Hot and Sour Seafood Soup 61
Sea Bass in a Coconut and Lime Reduction 120
Red Snapper en Papillote 124
Wok-Fried Chicken with Hot Basil 126
Chicken in Pandan Leaves 128

LONG BEANS
Wok-Fried Chicken with Hot Basil 126

M

MANGETOUT
Pad Thai 82

MANGO
Cambodian Mango Salad 72
Sea Bass in a Coconut and Lime Reduction 120

INDEX

P

PAK CHOY
Pad Thai 82

PEPPER (green, red, yellow)
Cambodian Mango Salad 72
Kampot Pepper Squid 78

PINEAPPLE
Khmer Rice Cakes 66
Chicken in Pandan Leaves 128
Roasted Pineapple 146

PRAWN
Breakfast Soup Guy Teaw 54
Rice Porridge Bor Bor 58
Hot and Sour Seafood Soup 60
Prawn Laksa 118
Sea Bass in a Coconut and Lime Reduction 120
Sautéed Prawns with Chili Relish 137

PORK
Breakfast Soup Guy Teaw 54
Rice Porridge Bor Bor 58
Pork with Chili Relish 132
Sweet Pork Belly 134

R

RICE (flour, noodles, steamed)
Rice Porridge Bor Bor 58
Khmer Rice Cakes 66
Pad Thai 82
Fish Amok 116
Prawn Laksa 118
Taro and Sticky Rice Pudding 150
Sticky Rice 152
Red Snapper with Green Curry 122
Wok-Fried Chicken with Hot Basil 126
Chicken in Pandan Leaves 128

S

SCALLOPS
Scallop Ceviche 76

SHIITAKE MUSHROOM
Pad Thai 82

SOFT-SHELL CRAB
Soft-Shell Crab Tempura 74

SPINACH
Lamb Cutles with Fresh Spinach 86

SQUID
Rice Porridge Bor Bor 58
Hot and Sour Seafood Soup 60
Kampot Pepper Squid 78

**STOCK
(chicken, pork or vegetable)**
Breakfast Soup Guy Teaw 54
Rice Porridge Bor Bor 58
Sweet Pork Belly 130

**STOCK
(fish and/or prawn)**
Hot and Sour Seafood Soup 60
Sea Bass in a Coconut and Lime Reduction 120

SWEET POTATO
Coconut-Smoked Rack of Lamb 136
Sweet Potato Pudding
with Tapioca 148

T

TARO
Taro and Sticky Rice Pudding 150

TOFU
Pad Thai 82

TOMATO
Cambodian Mango Salad 72
Beef Lok Lak 130

V

VERMICELLI NOODLES
Breakfast Soup Guy Teaw 54
Crispy Vermicelli 80

W

WATERMELON
Watermelon Salad 68

Y

YOGHURT
Watermelon Salad 68
Coconut-Smoked Rack of Lamb 136

IMPRINT

Published by Elsa Publishing, Munich 2021

Text
Text copyright © Kathleen Beringer, 2020
Recipes edited by Sylvia Goulding
for bookwise GmbH, Munich.

"The History of Khmer Cuisine" written by
Jonathon R. Ramsey, Hebron, U.S.A

Illustrations
All illustrations copyright © Claudia Lieb, Munich 2020

Photography
All photography copyright © Joerg Lehmann, 2020
culinaryworld.com / Instagram: @imagebay /
@thebreadtourist

On page 8–9, 47 photography copyright © Song Saa

Concept
© Agenten und Freunde, Munich 2020

Layout, lithography and production
01-digitale produktion, Oliver F. Meier, Munich

Print and postpress
aprinta druck GmbH, 86650 Wemding

Paper
150 g/m² Magno Volume

All rights reserved. Without limiting the rights under copyright reserved above, no part of this publication may be reproduced, stored in or introduced into a retrieval system, or transmitted in any form or by any means (electronic, mechanical, photocopying, recording or otherwise) without the prior written permission of both the copyright owner and the above publisher of this book.

elsapublishing.com

ISBN 978-3-948859-03-9

Printed in Germany